The
Mad Forties

The
Mad Forties

Grace Adams and Edward Hutter

Harper & Brothers Publishers
New York and London

THE MAD FORTIES

To W. P.

Contents

[vii]

Contents

The world is infested, just now, by a new sect of philosophers, who have not yet suspected themselves of forming a sect, and who, consequently, have adopted no name. They are the *Believers in everything Old*. . . . The only common bond among the sect, is Credulity:—let us call it Insanity at once, and be done with it. Ask any one of them *why* he believes this or that, and, if he be conscientious (ignorant people usually are), he will make you very much such a reply as Talleyrand made when asked *why* he believed in the Bible. "I believe in it first," said he, "because I am Bishop of Autun; and, secondly, *because I know nothing about it at all.*"

EDGAR ALLAN POE

The Mad Forties

I

Mary Gove Arrives at 47 Bond Street, New York

IN THE LATE AUTUMN OF 1844 THE STEAMBOAT FROM BOSTON LEISURELY RACED THE DAWN AROUND BATTERY Park, nosed in at Pier 1 North River, and settled in silence at the wharf. At the first half light a little sharp-faced woman in a gray bonnet, with a russet shawl wrapped tightly around her thin shoulders, stepped briskly from the Ladies' Cabin. When she saw several men sauntering around the deck, she shrank into a dark corner and sat on a stool. One of the men made two or three turns in her direction and then said, "A sharp morning, Miss. Have you the time of day?"

Fixing the man with a stare to match the chill of the morning, the lady returned to the smothering suffocation of the cabin. In our boasted land of freedom, she reflected bitterly, a poor woman wrapped in semi-Quaker garb, cowering and coughing in the corner of a steamship, is not secure from insult.

As she awoke her sleeping daughter she sniffed again the fetid air of the cabin and pondered regretfully over the lack of water her fellow travelers used on their bodies. Accompanied by the child she once more braved the deck, leaned on the railing next to the city, and surveyed the sleeping world.

The wooden wharf to which the boat was tied was unsubstantial, run-down and badly in need of paint, but beyond that the city gave a handsome and elegant appearance. Through the bare old trees of Battery Park she saw to the north of Bowling Green the brick buildings of red and gray, with white doors and windows and outside shutters a lively green. Above all loomed the spires of St. Paul's and Trinity Church.

As the sun rose there was a busy stir within the boat and on the wharf. Mother and daughter descended the gangplank into the confusion on the shore. Hoarse voices bawled, "Carriage, Sir," "Carriage, Madame," "United States," "Astor House," "City," and all the names of New York's twenty or more reputable hotels. Whips were crossed and the language that followed was ill-suited to the ears of a twelve-year-old.

The mother, clasping her daughter's hand tightly in her own, shrank back to the edge of the crowd, until she feared she would lose the last carriage. Then she gave her trunk to a black man. He was a pariah like herself, so she instinctively sought the sympathy of his services. He loaded them with the trunk into a lumbering sort of hybrid carriage, half stage and half hackney-coach, which was already crowded with other passengers. She consulted a letter drawn from her pocket and asked to be set down before Dr. Shew's Water Cure at 47

Bond Street. The driver whipped his horses and the carriage lurched forward.

From the wharf the horses trotted west on Battery Place to Bowling Green, then around the pretty little park and into Broadway, where they proceeded in a walk, for the ten-year-old macadam had grown rough and bumpy and the street was teeming. Even at this early hour the carts of butchers and bakers jostled along in the midst of handsome private carriages and the overcrowded omnibuses. Since bus fare had been reduced to two and three cents New Yorkers had developed such a distaste for walking that even laborers rode to their jobs.

The streets were dirty, with litter and heaps of garbage in the gutters. The brick houses, former residences which had been converted into shops and warehouses, were freshly painted, with awnings advertising their wares in front and the names of their proprietors set in metal disks in the sidewalk. Many of the shops had expensive plate glass windows, a constant temptation to the roving rowdies from the Five Points.

Greenery and spraying water came into view as they approached City Hall Park, the center and most exciting part of town. The little girl stared open-mouthed at Barnum's Museum, the Park Theater and the fabulous Astor House. Directly in front of the beautiful hotel was a spectacle that fascinated the mother above all others. It was the fountain from which columns of

[3]

water had spouted night and day since the Croton Works Reservoir had opened two years before.

At Prince Street the coach was empty of passengers save the woman and child, for most of the city's hotels were downtown. The Gothic buildings of New York University rose above the residences of Greenwich Village. Just beyond Bleeker they turned into Bond Street, which ran the one long block between Broadway and the Bowery, and drew up before 47.

The lady lost any feeling of sympathy she might have entertained for her fellow pariah when he demanded twelve shillings for her two-mile trip in his crowded old carriage. Fifty cents was enough, she felt, but she compromised on a dollar. She sighed in vexation. She hated to compromise on anything.

Number 47 was like the other houses in Bond Street, a well-kept four-story-and-basement residence. While the coachman conferred with the maid about the disposal of the trunk, a short broad man, with a large head and a high intellectual forehead, bustled to the door and extended his hand. "Welcome to our establishment," he said. "You are Mrs. Gove, aren't you?"

"Yes, and this is my daughter Elma. Come, dear, and greet Dr. Shew."

Dr. Shew led them into the front parlor and before Mrs. Gove had time to remove her shawl or drink the proffered glass of water from the maid, he began to talk. He told her about his practice and the journal for which he was writing and editing. He asked the news of her transcendental friends in New England. He deplored their talk of freeing the slaves and allowing them to remain in America. Colonization was the thing. Send all black blood back to Africa where it originated and belonged. He was tremendously pleased, though, that the transcendentalists were becoming interested in hygiene. Hygiene and colonization would be the salvation of America.

He was still declaiming, not allowing Mrs. Gove to slip in a word, when a young and beautiful woman filled the room like the sweep of a summer breeze. Her face was infantine in its sweetness, full of the beauty of the rose-bud just bursting into bloom. Her hair fell in masses of curls over her round white neck. A simple morning dress with no ornaments or covering but the curls disclosed that there were no corsets beneath. Her rich red lips parted smilingly as she clasped the visitor's hands in her own, kissed her, and sank beside her on the couch. "Mrs. Gove," she exclaimed warmly, "I have so long wished to know you."

Charmed as she was by Mrs. Shew, the newcomer was quick to detect a flaw in her husband. A man had been announced and Dr. Shew said, "Ladies, you will please leave the parlor. This gentleman and I wish to have some confidential conversation."

Mrs. Gove shot a questioning look at Mrs. Shew who was already placidly arising. Evidently she was accustomed to being ordered around. Mrs. Gove reflected, perhaps irrelevantly but certainly characteristically, "That man will never appear in my bedroom."

Rankled or not she was excited when Mrs. Shew led her over the house, while the maid directed Elma down the basement stairs and out into the back yard to the privy. Mrs. Shew showed first the office where Dr. Shew wrote his journal, then the conservatory which was her favorite room, the sleeping apartments upstairs, with the wonderful Croton water on every floor. Then came the pride of the house—the douche room. Its entire floor was covered by a shallow, square wooden tub, and the walls were festooned with pipes which sent varying streams of water cascading into the tub by the turn of a screw.

Mrs. Shew next took her guest to her own room and showed her lying naked on a blanket her chubby, rosy two-months-old son. If this wasn't the most publicized baby in the world, certainly he was the first ever intentionally delivered in a bath tub—even though it was a sitting-hip bath especially constructed for the purpose. Every detail of its gestation had been written up by the father from the moment the mother discovered her pregnancy till the day after its birth when she took a four-mile walk.

Finally Mrs. Shew brought Mrs. Gove and Elma to a bright room with windows on three sides in the el over the conservatory. Instead of a bed this room had two neat couches covered with pretty chintz, a rocking chair and two others, a closed washstand, and one of the prettiest little tables in all New York. A fire was glowing in the grate and the two travelers felt very happy.

When they went down to dinner at three o'clock Mrs. Gove realized from the voices coming from the kitchen that Dr. Shew was supervising the cooking of the meal, as every conscientious proprietor of a Water Cure must—to make sure that the cook does not slip butter or salt or heating spices or exciting condiments into the food, and that she lets it become cool before serving it.

In the center of the dining table was a large basket of biscuits made from Graham flour, and at each place there were two bare plates piled one upon the other. That was all, and while Mrs. Gove waited for the chilled food to be brought in she surveyed her fellow boarders.

A few of them rather sheepishly placed small parcels on the table and took from them rolls made of white flour and small pats of butter. Those who did this, Mrs. Gove was not surprised to note, had very every-day faces and wore conventional clothes—the men high stocks and tight cravats; the ladies close-fitting bodices, with their hair pulled back and pinned in wads on their heads. She had seen their like at Brattleboro and Lebanon Springs. They were paying to take the water cure but were too stupid to get the extra benefits of dress reform and hydropathic diet. The men of whom she approved wore flat collars open at the throat and flowing ties; the ladies like herself and Mrs. Shew had loose dresses and falling hair.

The maid brought in the first course, all in one large bowl. On each diner's plate Dr. Shew put a small piece of lean boiled meat, potatoes, carrots, turnips and cabbage. After this had been eaten the top plates were taken away and plain griddled cakes, covered with a slightly sweetened cream sauce, were placed on the bottom ones.

Mrs. Gove was pleased to see that the Shews followed the Priessnitz diet so carefully. From her experience and knowledge she was sure that this would be the dinner every day, except that sometimes the meat would be broiled and a special dish of sauerkraut or dumplings added, and that the dessert would be varied with rice and apple pudding.

She knew, too, that supper every night would be brown bread, sweet milk, buttermilk, sour milk, and potatoes boiled in their jackets. Breakfast would be the same, though if it were summer, fruit would be substituted for the potatoes. Mrs. Gove was also certain that like herself all her table companions were wearing wet girdles, that they all slept on hard mattresses, and opened their bedroom windows to varying heights according to the length of time they had been inured to night air.

The more conventional among them talked about the same topics that ordinary persons throughout the country were discussing—the possibility of war with Mexico;

James Polk's chances of beating Henry Clay in the coming election; the murder of Joseph Smith and his brother Hyram by a mob in Illinois; the state of Andrew Jackson's health; the fact that railroad collisions were becoming as frequent and fatal as steamboat explosions; the news sent back from England by Mr. Barnum that the Queen had invited General Tom Thumb to Buckingham Palace; the report that when Texas was annexed the Florida and Iowa territories would also be admitted as states; the inability of the volunteer hose companies to deal with the fires that were continually breaking out in New York and the congested mill towns of New England; the potato famine that was driving the Irish over here at the rate of 100,000 a year; the rumor that old Mr. Astor's annual income was $1,000,000; the completion of telegraphic communications all the way to Washington; the strike for higher wages by the carpenters of Philadelphia and the violence of the rent riots in New York State; Postmaster General Granger's calculation that 24,000,000 sheets of paper had been mailed in the United States within the year and his prediction that America might soon adopt the English custom of envelopes and adhesive stamps; the certainty that the new Grace Church, now almost completed at Broadway and Tenth Street, would be the handsomest in America, and the dry goods store that A. T. Stewart was erecting at Broadway and Chambers would be grander and more elegant than any mercantile establishment in the whole world.

Mrs. Gove was pleased to observe that all the persons, as conservative as many of them still were in their habits, had such a firm grasp of important national events. But the conversations that really warmed her heart were those carried on by her table companions who showed by their dress and their choice of words that they lived the art life.

They praised the Italian Opera Company's performance of *Le Barbier de Seville* in Castle Garden, where the old fort had been converted into a theater seating 8,000. They remarked how much more hygienic were the three hundred select young ladies who went regularly to Madame Hawley's Institution of Gymnastic Exercises than the young gentlemen of the town who confined their exercise to sitting at desks in Wall Street and strolling Broadway, befouling the air with the smoke from their cigars. They deplored Horace Greeley's attempt to make Fourierism, which was essentially the philosophy of artists and aesthetes, into a workingman's ideology. They argued hotly over whether Eugene Sue, Dumas, George Sand or Disraeli would be judged by posterity the greatest novelist of the nineteenth century. They debated with equal passion whether darkening the lashes and brows with henna was in as good taste as whitening the skin with rice powder. They all agreed that Mrs. Frances Osgood in her volume, *The Flowers of Poetry and the Poetry of*

Flowers, had finally married art and science in exquisite perfection. They agreed, too, that Mrs. Cora Mowatt's *Fashion* was the most urbane play ever produced in America, though several suspected that Epes Sargeant had written not only its prologue but its every act and scene. They referred discreetly to the stupidity of the manager of Niblo's Garden Theatre who had refused admittance to a visiting French countess accompanied by her maid, because he thought two females coming unattended to the play could only hail from the Five Points. They deemed it absurd for Henry James and Ralph Waldo Emerson to dare argue the fine points of reincarnation with a man as famed for his learning as Professor George Bush. They said that the pleasantest results of faster rail and steamship service was that it allowed New Yorkers to enjoy bananas and visitors all the year round.

Mrs. Gove, listening quietly to these stimulating discussions as she gnawed her cold potatoes, sighed with delight. New York was surely a broader and happier place than any city in New England. Boston might be the Hub, but New York was indeed the City of the Whirlpool.

II

The English Intellectuals
Discover America

IN THE 1820'S AMERICA BEGAN TO BE
DISCOVERED BY THE ENGLISH IN-
TELLECTUALS. BLUE-EYED FRANCES
Wright was in the vanguard of the explorers and the
report on her wanderings as far west as the Mississippi
was published in London. She had seen the New World
and it worked! Her ecstaticisms over the trying ground
set the pattern for all future findings by the members
of her set.

Poor Mrs. Trollope, a family friend, was beguiled
by Frances to a fantastic wilderness outside of Memphis
under the certainty of making a quick fortune by open-
ing a kind of department store. Two years later, her
money gone and living with her two ill children on the
grudging charity of friends, the luckless woman started
writing her American wanderings down as the one
chance of making some money. Her book, *Domestic
Manners of the Americans,* was the detailed story of
her buffetings about by the frontiersmen suspicious of
her English county background. The book displeased
Americans; but it enraged the English intellectuals.

They felt that she had betrayed the liberal cause, that one should not disclose flaws in a democracy under the flimsy excuse that such flaws were present. They wrote in their journals that she was venal, vulgar and a Tory underneath, and succeeding visitors did their best to erase the blot of the brave old woman.

Harriet Martineau took it upon herself as a special mission. She was well suited to her task. She was famous in England as a writer of fictionalized economics and brought over enough letters to open every door in America. In addition, she was providentially equipped for frontier traveling by possessing only 40 per cent of the standard equipment of senses; for besides being deaf she could neither taste nor smell. As no one would bother to shout anything disagreeable into her ear trumpet she heard only what Americans, anxious to please a distinguished visitor, thought advisable.

Harriet, on her part, met them more than halfway, even to the extent of changing her table manners; switching her knife and fork from hand to hand in the peculiar, affected manner of plain American people. Mrs. Trollope, though violently anti-slavery, had been forced to admit that life in the South was more agreeable to her than in the North, while Harriet could not be seduced by either plantation or spa. Sleeping calmly in crawling beds and ignoring the amber flood of country-wide tobacco spit, she devoted her scored senses to the one idea of intellectual rapprochement between England and America. A startling example recorded by her was the tale of the Redcoats who on their way to burn Washington reverently tipped their hats as they marched by Mt. Vernon.

Abolition was not fashionable in the 1830's even in New England. It was new and violent with William Lloyd Garrison's assertion that "the constitution of the United States is a covenant with death and an agreement with hell and should be annulled." Consequently when abolitionists began grabbing for the loose end of the speaking tube Harriet's admirers began to dwindle, until only the firebrands were left.

For all her intentions and strivings to please, the book about her travels aroused more bitter comment in many sections of America than had the Trollope she had set out to erase. In England, however, Harriet's book was a complete success. She became the undisputed authority on America and on its individual inhabitants. Her intellectual followers listened greedily to her discoveries of mental cousins across the water.

One of these was a young man named Bronson Alcott who had a unique school in Boston. In rooms tastily decorated with exalted sculpture and paintings he had discarded the disciplinary methods common to more austere and drab institutions. Alcott held that the chief function of a teacher was not to teach but to assist his students in "obeying the impulses of their own nature." Accordingly in his own Temple School he encouraged his tiny charges to ask questions about subjects generally considered beyond their understanding, and to become interested in the love life of the birds and bees and, to a certain extent, those images of God called men. Under such creative tutelage, Alcott had assured Miss Martineau, quite ordinary little boys were budding into geniuses as wise as Plato, and more artistic.

In London Mr. J. T. Greaves was particularly interested in hearing of these progressive methods, for he had once stayed for several years in Switzerland where, though they knew no common language in which to converse, he and Pestolozzi had become intuitively very close. Mr. Greaves now wrote to Alcott and asked if his modern technique did not reflect the spiritual influence of the Swiss master.

Alcott replied by return packet that he was indeed employing Pestolozzi's concepts in his Temple School, and through them he was calling forth the essential lives of his students' souls and fitting them for manifestations in literature, art and philosophy. Mr. Greaves was so impressed that he fired the enthusiasm of a group of young English Mystics who joined him in founding a similar institution at Ham Common in Surrey. As was fitting, they named it Alcott House and invited its inspiration to visit it.

Bronson Alcott during his entire life never had any money of his own, and whenever the incessant occasions arose when money was needed he called on his friends. This time it was Emerson who gave him the money for the trip, and in 1842 Alcott sailed for England.

From Ham Common he wrote to his cousin William

Alcott, who was an ardent follower of the dietary theories of Sylvester Graham, that William would be especially pleased with the school because its thirty children were made to bathe each morning and were allowed no food except fruits, vegetables and plain bread, and no drink but water. The person responsible for this improvement over the Temple School's regimen was the headmaster of Alcott House, a youth in his twenties named Henry Gardener Wright.

This Mr. Wright, Alcott assured his cousin, "possesses more genius for teaching than any person I have yet seen . . . he impersonates and realizes my own ideas of education and is the first person I have met that has entered into this divine art of inspiring human clay, and moulding it into the stature and image of divinity . . . I am already knit to him by more than human ties, and must take him with me to America, as a coadjutor in our high vocation or else remain here with him. But I hope to effect the first."

And to Emerson concerning this remarkable young man, Bronson Alcott wrote, "You have never seen his like—so deep and serene, so clear, so true, so good . . . (Alcott House) is like my own school except a wiser wisdom and a lovelier love presides. . . . He cherishes hopes of making our land the place of his experiment in human culture and of proving to others the worth of the divine idea that now fills and exalts him."

When Alcott returned to America the next year, he not only took Mr. Wright with him but another reformer, Charles Lane, and a thousand of their books. This library was discussed and pictured. Margaret Fuller listed the titles in the *Dial* for the guidance of its readers in buying books for themselves. She declared it to be the finest, richest collection of mystic literature in America.

Mr. Lane's love may not have been so lovely as Mr. Wright's nor his wisdom so wise, but certainly his will was more indomitable, as the Alcott family discovered the moment he came to live with them. Daughter Louisa May remembered Charles Lane with bitterness all her life. He was the one, however, who possessed the $1800 essential for buying the land upon which Mr. Wright was to prove to others the worth of the divine idea that exalted him. For by now the original idea of Mr. Alcott and Mr. Wright combining their geniuses into a super school for children had developed into the determination to make on some New England farm a New Eden for adults.

As soon as they arrived in America Alcott proudly exhibited his two English Mystics to his transcendental friends in Concord, Boston, Lynn and Lexington. Mr. Lane was bargaining for a farm near Harvard, Massachusetts, he announced, and the New Life would soon begin.

The principles governing this paradise on earth would be love and freedom. Love and freedom for the whole world—mankind, animals, the very ground itself. There would be no violence in this Eden, and no subjugating

or exploiting. Animals would not be killed for food nor
would they be used as beasts of burden. All the tilling
of the soil would be done with spades by the hands of
the men who would eat the fruits of the soil. And no
fertilizer would be used, for that would mean forcing
the ground unnaturally. The crops as soon as they
ripened would be spaded under again so that the very
fruits themselves, with the exception of those required
for immediate use, could re-enrich the earth from which
they had sprung. No materials would be used whose
production might violate the principles of this dream.

Leather shoes could not be worn, nor silken garments,
for that would necessitate severally the violent death of
cattle and the exploitation of silk worms. Woolen cloth
was out, too, because its manufacture would deprive the
sheep of the covering which nature in her bounty had
given them. Cotton cloth was tabooed, also, because it
was produced by black brothers in bondage. Oil lamps
to Mr. Alcott meant only death to the whales. Only a
diet of fruits and vegetables would be eaten and only
linen garments worn. Candles must be made from
vegetable fats. As for shoes—well, as soon as those
which the dreamers already owned wore out, they must
think up a way to fashion new ones from bark. Or,
better still, go barefooted. Bare feet and linen garments
even in a New England winter would not be unen-
durable, Bronson Alcott was sure, because the warm
love of angels descending into men's hearts would
ameliorate the climate about them. Soon the bland air

of Eden would envelop the whole planet and the atmosphere of Harvard, Massachusetts, become so tempered that even oranges would grow there.

When the heavenly planners brought this message to Lynn their host was the Reverend Mr. Robbins, the local Unitarian minister. To honor the high-thinking trio he threw a tremendous picnic and invited all the neighboring intellectuals. Cake, ice-cream and lemonade were as abundant as exalted phrases, but not the home-made wine that was usual at such festivities, for the guests like the Reverend Mr. Robbins were Temperance.

At the picnic Mr. Wright, pursuing his interest in youth, was attracted to a pretty child of about ten years. She told him that her name was Elma Penn Gove and led him by the hand to her mother, who was standing apart from the others. Mr. Wright wondered why this was, especially when after she began to talk he found Mrs. Gove to be by far the most interesting woman he had met in America.

Not only was she well versed in the sciences of phrenology and mesmerism, but in the cause of woman's emancipation she had made gestures more conspicuous than those achieved by the most ardent of English feminists. When after moving from New Hampshire to Massachusetts she had learned from the advanced friends she made there that a white woman had as much right as a black man to call her soul her own, she hadn't just quietly left her husband. She had sent *him* packing back to their native backwoods, while she stayed firmly in Lynn. This novel behavior had caused several New England papers to which she contributed verses to put her on their black list, but had made her a good draw on the lesser lecture circuits from Rhode Island to Ohio.

Her best show had been in Philadelphia where, co-starring with John Greenleaf Whittier who stuck to his old anti-slavery routine, she had demonstrated the need for dress reform. Before a mixed audience, composed in part of professors from the University of Pennsylvania, and using her own person as her model, she had shown the effect of tight lacing upon the female form. The members of her own sex among her listeners had called for restorative salts and fainted. The ensuing excitement had been so great that even New York editors got wind of it and James Gordon Bennett wrote spitefully about her motives.

Being denounced by a scandal-loving toady to the reactionary middle class enhanced Mary Gove's stature among the liberals. But just before Mr. Wright met her she had got into disfavor with her own kind over an important point of doctrine. At an abolitionist gathering she had interrupted William Lloyd Garrison to declare: "The Northern wife is worse off than the Southern slave, for her mental cultivation gives her a keenness of anguish that the want of spiritual culture saves her Southern sister from." The dressing down that Garrison gave her for this unorthodoxy caused her to say that Mr. Garrison must be called a great humanitarian simply because he lacked all human traits.

Mr. Wright well knew what heresy it was to the liberal cause for a white person of either sex to claim to be able to suffer as exquisitely as those of darker hues. Yet he was so overcome by the magnetism of Mrs. Gove's personality that he invited her to sit with him and the speakers from Concord at the Conversations which were to finish off the picnic.

This sympathetic attention, together with Mr. Wright's beautiful seeming and the spheres of benign influence that kept radiating from him to her, so inspired Mrs. Gove that after Alcott and Emerson and Channing had conversed loftily about the Nature of Prophecy, Duty, Freedom, Peace, Abolition, Non-resistance, Metachemistry, and International Non-intervention, she, though not on the planned program, arose to speak. She spoke, so she said, as though possessed by the very angels. The drift of her discourse was that conventional marriage was the "annihilation of woman, the grave of her beauty, and often the end of her health and usefulness."

The transcendentalists, carried away by her eloquence, congratulated her warmly when she sat down. But the next day, after they realized the import of her speech, they were pointedly cool to her. Mrs. Gove contended afterwards that in this declaration she had just been a bit ahead of her time. And it rankled her particularly when she recalled that when Women's Rights later became popular in this same region "the most distinguished citizen of Concord" bought this very same speech from her and published it as his own.

III

Mystics and Dieticians, Love and Morality and Spheres of Divine Influence

THE BEAUTIFUL SEEMING AND THE SPHERES OF DIVINE INFLUENCE WHICH SMOTE MRS. GOVE boomeranged back to Mr. Wright, and he began to show traits that had not been apparent in Surrey. He exhibited a fondness for sweets, used violet water on his handkerchiefs, and spent a lot of time, that might better have been devoted to spiritual meditation, making waves and ringlets in his long hair with a wet brush. In short, he appeared to be, as Mr. Lane characterized him, a small fop and a dandy.

This was very distressing to Bronson Alcott, who deplored the frivolity that his dear friends Emerson and Hawthorne and Margaret Fuller descended to when they stayed at Brook Farm. The laughter and singing at West Roxbury seemed to him almost as regrettable as the fact that the Brook Farmers, to a certain extent, supported themselves by degrading means. They acted as servants and slaves to a large herd of cows—fed them, policed them, and sold their milk in Boston.

For his part, Mr. Wright was dismayed by the impractical, ascetic heights to which his vision of a paradise on earth had been carried by Mr. Lane. With all its other virtues, the plan for Fruitlands, as they had decided to call their farm, lacked two which Mr. Wright considered essential to happiness—beauty and reason. He pointed out to Mr. Lane that while they waited for the warmth of men's hearts to spread out and then down into the soil, and flowers to replace pig-sties, they would freeze and starve to death. And they would surely be unaesthetic sights to one another's eyes flopping about in the rough clothes they might weave if the climate ever tempered enough for them to grow their own flax.

Furthermore, Mr. Wright declared that while he waited for nature to become improved by the communal love of all men, he meant to improve that part of it, himself, with which he personally had to deal. Specifically he intended to cook and flavor plain New England beans and sour New England apples in any manner that would make them taste less abhorrent. "I would reject the deathly complications of the world as it is," he explained grandly, "but I will still live an Art Life."

These sentiments, Mr. Lane replied, showed only "folly, vanity and degeneracy."

Such altercations between the two English Mystics went on interminably, in the Alcott household and wherever the plans for Fruitlands were discussed, even in Conversations which were aimed at recruiting new

[23]

members for the paradise on earth. Bronson Alcott was miserable, but he tried not to take sides.

Finally one morning, when Mr. Lane tried to strike Mr. Wright because he insisted on pouring cream on his oatmeal, Mr. Alcott realized that he had to take a stand. His principles forced him into Mr. Lane's corner. For one mortal to threaten another with physical violence was, of course, wrong, but not so wicked as for a grown man to deprive a helpless little calf of the very best of its mother's milk. Mr. Wright forthwith left Mr. Alcott's house.

Once outside he realized that he no longer had a home in America, or any money. All his savings had been invested in his passage and in his share of the richest mystic library in the New World.

He walked from Concord to Lynn and to the small house with the white muslin curtains where Mrs. Gove, after kicking out her husband, still lived. It was late when he got there. Though she was alone Mrs. Gove welcomed him cordially and showed him to the guest room. Then she returned to her own room and sat alone in the darkness, looking out of the window and thinking how wonderful it was to have under her roof a gentleman so different from that boorish Hiram Gove.

After a while the darkness was pierced by the beam of a candle and Mr. Wright stood beside her. Mrs. Gove's first thought was "What will the neighbors think?"—for muslin curtains are thin. For this Mr. Wright rebuked her. Though he was several years her junior he called her a child. He accused her of being a slave to the conventions of a world that she professed to despise.

"Darling," he said solemnly, stroking her hair as she sat at his feet, "love is the fulfilling of the law. Morality is a widespread disease."

It is difficult for anyone, let alone Mrs. Gove, to have a good word to say about disease, so she allowed him to free her from "the bonds of false morality, a virtue that spreads over the world a pall of death."

In after years Mary Gove looked back upon this night with shame; not because she had accepted Mr. Wright's faith so readily, but because she later was repentant. "At dawn," she wrote, "I drew myself away from that great, true and loving heart, and went alone, and in darkness, to pray God to forgive me for one of the truest, purest and holiest acts of my life."

During the weeks that he stayed with her, and waited for his return fare to be sent out from England, Mr. Wright told his hostess other of his beliefs and experiences. She was particularly interested in the pilgrimage he had made to the Miracle Man of the Sudetes.

Vincent Priessnitz was an untutored, simple-mannered peasant who lived halfway up a mountain in Austrian Silesia, a region abounding in gushing springs and limpid streams. One day while cutting wood in the forest he happened to chop his leg, and to staunch the blood he stuck it in the nearest spring. The wound healed in record time. After this whenever any of his

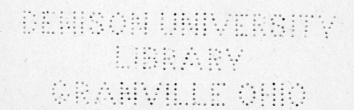

family felt indisposed from any cause he would hustle them off to running water for a dousing of the afflicted part. Soon his neighbors were responding so favorably to enforced immersion that Vincent Priessnitz began to be spoken of as a healer by his fellow mountaineers, and to get into trouble with the law.

The physicians of the region sued him for practicing medicine without a license; the storekeeper who had a monopoly on selling drugs to the community accused him of doping the sponge with which he swabbed his patients. When the charges against him had grown almost as high as his mountain they were sent to Vienna for settlement.

The Austrian Government dispatched to the Sudetes an investigating commission which reported unanimously that Priessnitz was using no illegal drugs. The majority of these gentlemen added the information that he was also doing his patients no good. The dissenting opinion was handed down by the only non-medical man on the commission, the doddering but still influential Baron Turkheim, who gave it as his considered opinion that Vincent Priessnitz was the "most successful healer in all human history."

The Man of the Mountain was allowed to continue his baptisms; and soon the Baron's fashionable friends began making the tedious pilgrimage to Grafenberg. The fad spread to all the capitals of Europe and eventually across the English Channel and the Atlantic Ocean, and the community thrived. Accommodating the bewildered pilgrims provided work and money for everyone. From miles around peasant women would come to the resort ostensibly to sell fruit but mostly to bootleg cooked food to the ravenous guests.

By the time Mr. Wright went there in 1841 there were twenty cottages in the colony and a tremendous communal building where the five hundred patients ate. Among them were professors, advocates, diplomats, military men of all grades, at least a hundred counts and barons, ten princes and princesses, one archduchess, one heir to a reigning monarch, and ladies of fashion from every important capital.

These distinguished personages spent most of their time at Grafenberg squatting under water falls, sitting in pools, dipping their hands into springs and their feet into brooks, but Priessnitz bossed them even when they were dry. He made them give up all liquors, tobacco, tea and coffee; eat only the plainest foods; and take lots of exercise; for it was his theory that "the sluggard, the gourmand and the inebriate cannot have health at any price," and that "it is always the weak and enervated who are the most sensual and debased."

There was still another axiom of Priessnitz's that impressed Mrs. Gove especially. This was: "Live upon brown bread and water, if you desire the best cure." The reason it so excited her was that several years before, over here in America, Sylvester Graham had propounded a similar rule of health. "Human beings may subsist from childhood to extreme old age and possess the greatest muscular power," he had pronounced, "on good potatoes and water alone."

Graham, whose official position was that of Temperance Agent for Pennsylvania, had also ordered his followers to lay off all stimulants and wash their clothes and their persons. And he had promoted whole wheat bread so successfully that Graham flour and Graham crackers could now be purchased in all the better shops. Back in 1840, in one of the clairvoyant visions with which she had been gifted since girlhood, Mary Gove had foreseen the year 1940 proclaim Sylvester Graham the greatest scientist of the ages. Weren't his theories, she now asked Mr. Wright, identical with Priessnitz's?

To a certain extent Graham's and Priessnitz's teachings were similar, Mr. Wright conceded rather testily. But Priessnitz was more than just a dietician. He was a healer. Of course there was that other commission of reactionary physicians, this one sent out from Paris, who declared that water, except as a simple cleansing agent had nothing to do with his cures. All of his patients, these French obstructionists had asserted, were roués, gourmands and sots. It was the fresh air of the Sudetes, the wholesome diet and the regular habits which made them feel better. But Mr. Wright, and all those who had the proper attitude toward such matters, knew differently. It was the mystic properties that Priessnitz had discovered in water, and the miraculous ways by which he applied it, which effected his cures.

Mrs. Gove was glad indeed to learn that for once her

visions might have led her astray, and that Graham was not to become the world's greatest scientist, for he had expressed another sentiment which she, now that she thought of it, did not approve at all. In his "Lectures to Young Men on Chastity" the Pennsylvania Temperance Agent had spoken almost as slightingly of the "indulgence of the natural passion" as of coffee and cigars. Mary Gove now said solemnly to Henry Wright, "You have convinced me that Priessnitz is indeed the savior of the world. I am ready to accept the Water Cure." Afterwards, to prove that her conversion from Grahamism to hydropathy had been complete, she always explained when "Dr. Graham" was mentioned in her presence that he was a doctor "by courtesy only," and that, anyway, he seldom practiced what he preached.

The weeks that Mr. Wright spent with Mrs. Gove were filled with Love and Beauty and much high conversation, but they were not free of pain. Although they both bathed often, refrained from all stimulants and condiments, and from meat, too, because meat-eaters turned themselves into mausoleums of the dead, he continued to suffer excruciatingly from the tumor which had taken him to Grafenberg.

Finally it got so bad that Mrs. Gove went over to Concord and, scrupulously avoiding the Alcott home, begged enough money from friends there to pay for an operation. True to his Priessnitzian principles, Mr. Wright refused to be drugged even then, but asked Mrs. Gove to mesmerize him. Sitting on a plain chair, with his head pressed tight against her magnetic breast, he let the surgeon hack away at him. Even that did little good. Friends came from England to take him home to die.

After she had spent his last week in America with him at a hotel in New York, and bade him a soulful farewell at the boat, Mrs. Gove returned to Lynn to learn just what price she must pay for letting Mr. Wright free her from the bonds of a false morality. For now the townspeople had the evidence of their own eyes—or at least those of one curious villager who had peeped through the muslin curtains more than once—to back up Hiram Gove's assertion that his wife bore watching.

Even Mrs. Robbins, the Unitarian minister's wife, turned her head when they passed on the street. When the children brought around their May baskets that spring, they left one at her door. But on it was scrawled the ugliest words they knew: "Grass widow." When she went out on her lecture tour, boardinghouse keepers either shut their doors in her face or packed her out in fury, depending on just when they heard the news about her. Ladies turned their backs to her and ostentatiously shielded their babies from her gaze. Even her own family agreed that her husband was right in taking Elma from her.

But Mary Gove wasn't downed. As she sought out one boardinghouse after another she continued to take her baths, eat her natural food, and repeat the facts about water cure that Mr. Wright had taught her, for now she had decided to dedicate her life to his memory by bringing health and happiness to others through the magic agency of water. She also thought that hydropathy might be of some help to the lung trouble with which she had been afflicted since infancy. As if in answer to a prophecy she learned that a Water Cure was being established in Vermont. She went there at once.

The Brattleboro Water Cure House was an expensive place. Even when one patient shared a room with another his board alone was $10.00 a week. Medical attendance and the use of the outdoor baths added another $5.00 weekly, and there were many other extras. Mrs. Gove could not afford to live in the establishment and undergo a full course of treatments, herself, as anyone entering a new branch of healing always should. But she got board in a private home in the village for $3.50 and gave lectures in the sciences to the ladies taking the cure to raise the fees for the baths.

While she was at Brattleboro she came across a copy of the *Water Cure Journal and Herald of Reform*, edited by Dr. Joel Shew, the head of a rival establishment over at Lebanon Springs in New York State. He, though a graduate physician, had made the pilgrimage to Grafenberg just as had Mr. Wright. Mrs. Gove decided that she must transfer to Lebanon Springs immediately.

By the time she got there Dr. Shew had already left for New York City to found the first urban Water Cure in the world. Though she was disappointed not to see him, his absence was really a break for Mrs. Gove. The physician who was to take Dr. Shew's place had not yet showed up. Because of her experience at Brattleboro she was gratefully received by the manager who hired her temporarily, but instantaneously, as resident physician.

But the thought of practicing hydropathy in New York had already fired Mrs. Gove's imagination. Dr. Shew, she learned, had discovered that the new Croton water, though not quite so pristine as that of the Sudetes, was the purest liquid in America. And while it was sometimes difficult to get patients to come to the country for the cure, the restless residents of New York were always looking for good boardinghouses; one which added hydropathy to its regular services should attract a crowd. Moreover, the metropolis offered thousands of potential patients who might pay a reasonable fee to be treated in their own homes.

And besides all this, Mrs. Gove remembered that no one in New York had called her harsh names during the week that she stayed there with Mr. Wright; and she had heard that in that progressive city kindly judges allowed the children of broken homes to live with whichever parent they desired. Perhaps New York held the solution to all her problems.

As soon as she had saved a little money she crossed over into New England for the last time. Elma was now living with some friends of her father's near their old

home in New Hampshire. The guardians refused to let
her mother see her or even send her a note. But one
afternoon as the child was gathering nuts some distance
from the house, a neighbor handed her a letter. Recog-
nizing her mother's handwriting she eagerly followed
him to a side road where Mrs. Gove waited in a buggy.
Hysterically happy in their reunion, they started off on
a dramatic, rain-drenched, all-night drive to Boston.
The next day they boarded the boat for New York.

IV

Water, Water Everywhere . . .

WATER, ACCORDING TO THE HY-DROPATHISTS, WAS THE MOST FORMIDABLE AS WELL AS THE purest of all natural elements. Not only could it tear ships apart and destroy the proudest of man's handi-works, it was the only power except God's own wrath forceful enough to rend rocks asunder. It was, indeed, next to man, the most favored of all His creations. Was it tokay or claret or sherry or porter or rum or even tea or coffee that God placed in the Garden of Eden? Dr. Shew would ask those of his patients who grew re-bellious at being kept on that one powerful but uninter-esting beverage.

And as for those foolish people who thought that the best way to cure themselves by water was to rush off to some fashionable place like Saratoga or the White Sulphur Springs and lie around all day in warm, evil-smelling pools—why, the very idea was horrifying. The water at those places was not pure. How could it be? It was drugged with sulphur and iron and lime-stone and all manner of unknown and probably mis-chievous elements. It was very nearly as tainted as the water in the old wells of Manhattan, polluted as they were by the seepage from graveyards and privies. And the man or woman who succumbed to those fake cures and went back to them year after year was forming habits just as insidious and deadly as drinking spirits, inhaling nicotine or taking morphine. It was only pure water that would do the work and then only under a trained hydropathist's exact prescription—because an element as potent as pure water could do inestimable mischief if taken by the wrong method or in improper doses.

The easiest way to absorb water into the system was by drinking it, but many people did so intemperately and inadvisedly. Dr. Shew was broad-minded enough about the matter to concede that there might be something to Dr. William Alcott's contention that thirst was really an abnormal appetite. Dr. Alcott had proved this to his own satisfaction by going for a whole year without taking a single drop of water, in spite of the formidable task of scaring out the necessary fruit juices in wintry New England. So although Dr. Shew administered water orally for hiccups, toothache, skin eruptions, palpitation of the heart and fatigue, and recommended the swallowing of lumps of ice for bleeding of the stomach, he cautioned his patients against drinking unthinkingly, especially while subjected to other processes of water cure, or at meals, when the action of so powerful an agent upon the chemistry of foods was unpredictable. Altogether, when it was necessary to inject water into the human body Dr. Shew preferred the enema. He worked hard to overcome his patients' aversion to that instrument. He assured them that it was in no wise painful, but decidedly agreeable, and that its use several times each day would not only insure a lady's health but add greatly to the charm of her presence.

The best method of getting water within the human system, however, was not abruptly through orifices but gradually through the skin. The process of cutaneous absorption the hydropathists called "exomosis" or "transudation" and they held it to be so easily provable that they would not waste time arguing about it with unbelievers.

The most popular way of inducing transudation was by means of the wet sheet. It was because they felt that to keep really fit they must be put into a wet sheet at least once a day that sincere devotees of water cure, like Mrs. Gove, always carted so much bedding around with them. The proper adjustment of the wet sheet required the services of several attendants. On a bed equipped with a hard mattress, or on the floor, they spread several thick woolen blankets evenly and smoothly and upon them they laid a large cotton or linen sheet which had just been dipped in cold water. The patient then stretched himself full length on the sheet and the attendants wound it tight about him. Then they folded the blankets as tautly around the sheet and secured them with large pins and tapes. Over the whole they threw a fat feather bed. According to the physical condition of the patient, his sensitiveness to water, and various other factors, he stayed in the casing from twenty-five minutes to several hours. The wet sheet was used for reducing all fevers, for toning up the body generally and, by ladies, for whitening the skin—for water had bleaching properties as well as healing and invigorating ones.

For out-patients who could not afford the attendants necessary for winding the sheet, and who slept alone, Dr. Shew recommended as a substitute the wet dress— a nightgown made with extra wide sleeves. But he warned all his subjects to beware of drinking water while incased in either the wet dress or the sheet. Such combinations worked serious mischief.

After the patient was out of his wet sheet or dress he was ready for his bath. At a well-conducted water cure house his choice of types of baths was almost endless. The most powerful of all was the shower. Though Dr. Shew boasted that he himself had probably taken as many as a hundred showers, he seldom prescribed that forcible remedy. Instead he preferred the douche bath, whose potency was about that of Croton oil. And he always cautioned his patients to keep a crouching position when under the douche, for water falling upon the head could be extremely dangerous. If it became necessary to immerse the head, then a special head bath should be taken, with the patient stretched flat on his back and turning his head from side to side in shallow water.

Many persons had the erroneous idea that because of

its name the head bath was the proper treatment for headaches. But this was far too energetic a remedy for so simple a malady and was used (and then not until all other means had failed) only in such serious illnesses as deafness, loss of the senses of taste and smell, delirium tremens and inflammation of the brain. Prolonged insanity indicated the need of a plunge or cold air bath. If the insane patient refused to plunge voluntarily into deep water or to stand naked in a hard wind, the most hazardous of all practices, that of dashing water at him, had to be resorted to.

For headaches as well as tooth- and earaches, gout and bleeding of the womb, the opposite of the head bath was usually recommended. Warm foot baths were also suitable for pains and aches of a nervous character. Other partial baths for lesser ailments were: the leg and arm bath for ulcers, rheumatism, sprains and wounds; hand baths for warts; mouth baths (instead of the customary clipping) for elongation of the palate; and, finally, for stomach and liver complaints, diseases of the bowels, womb and spine, piles, leucorrhea and inflammation of the chest, the most popular of all, the sitz bath. A person taking the sitz bath sat in water that was just deep enough to cover his abdomen, and only that part of him which was actually immersed was bare. Otherwise he was clothed as usual. With his head, trunk, arms and legs sticking out at strange angles, he stayed in the sitz bath from twenty to thirty minutes, depending upon how long he could keep his balance.

In the first water cure establishments in America, as well as at Priessnitz's colony, all baths were taken out-of-doors in running water. Cascades and water falls provided natural showers and douches. Springs and brooks were dammed up to form pools of the proper depths for the partial baths. The groves and ravines of the rural establishments presented arresting sights on bright summer days with patients lying, stooping, squatting and wallowing about in the brooks and rivulets—though bright screens and awnings usually prevented the curious from peering too closely at the ladies when any considerable portion of their bodies was jutting out of the water.

After Dr. Shew discovered that Croton water was superior in purity to any other in America he had rooms and vessels constructed that simulated the natural cascades and pools. At 47 Bond Street a patient could get every kind of wetting except the wave bath—and that did not really matter because its effect was precisely that of the douche.

For those who wanted to apply water at home but had neither the equipment nor the leisure for the more sedentary methods, Dr. Shew recommended several other forms of bathing. The mildest and most convenient was in his opinion the dripping sheet with which one or more attendants scrubbed the victim vigorously for five minutes. He called special attention to the towel bath because of its neatness. The skillful wielder of a towel could cleanse himself all over from a single quart of water without doing the least damage to the nicest carpeted room. Other quick baths were the sponge and the bath by affusion. The patient taking the latter stood in a wash tub, or in any convenient receptacle, and poured water over his neck and shoulders from a pitcher, cup or hand basin. For those who were unused to water, except on their hands and faces, Dr. Shew prepared a brief instructive pamphlet on "How to Bathe."

The guests at the water cure house interspersed these rapid baths among the more leisurely ones. They also had a great deal of water close to their skin even when fully clothed. The most popular form of undercover transudation was the wet girdle, made of rough toweling and soaked freshly every three hours. The regulation length of the wet girdle was three yards, but persons especially sensitive to water were allowed to wear slightly shorter ones and sometimes, in very cold weather, a piece of flannel on top of the toweling. Some physicians made their patients wear their girdles night and day. But Dr. Shew estimated their potency to be about the same as that of calomel or blood letting, and considered twenty-four hours of such strenuous treatment a little too much for the average constitution. So the only patients of his that wore their girdles at night were those whose business took them too far from water to keep them properly moist during the daytime.

Persons with weak lungs were advised to wear wet jackets above their girdles, and those who suffered from deep internal pains to use compresses of varying sizes and temperatures. These forms of exomosis had the added power of fomentation. They drew disease from far within the body to the surface of the skin. Whenever eruptions, sores and boils appeared beneath the compresses, jackets and girdles, a good hydrotherapist congratulated his patient and predicted a swift recovery. He knew that his remedies were effective.

These were the methods with which Dr. Shew treated the guests at 47 Bond Street and those who summoned him to their homes. In his *Water Cure Journal and Herald of Reform* and in his *Water Cure Manual,* which he re-edited and re-issued every year, he described how they could be successfully employed in the treatment of pneumonia, nephritis, stones in the bladder, asthma, worms, ships fever, smallpox, typhus fever— in fact, every ailment that more conventional physicians treated by laudanum, leeches, calomel, Cox's Hive Syrup, Croton oil, blood letting and cupping. Yet his reports of his cases were at first unexciting when compared with those of Priessnitz. Priessnitz had cured Polish generals of consumption, French marquises of broken spines, Russian grand dukes of apoplexy, while Dr. Shew had to be content with such items as these: putting a wet sheet around the little daughter of Mr. Joseph Allen of MacDougal Street who had a bad cold; placing wet bandages on the neck and wet towels on the lower limbs of the three-year-old son of Mr. Osborne of Grand Street who had been exposed to measles; giving three injections of a quart each to sixty-nine-year-old Mrs. Riley, three days since from Ireland, who had got cholera morbus from eating salt mackerel; showing Mrs. Gors who ran a boardinghouse down on Vesey Street how to take a bath with affusion; treating Mr. Perry of Orchard Street for frost bite and an Intelligent Lady of Fourth Street for warts.

The only really startling reports in the journal were those of which Mrs. Shew was the subject. She was an inexhaustible case. Her mother had died of consumption and though both her father and grandfather were physicians, they were not water curists. She had been allowed to lace tightly, to pile her hair on her head, eat several meats for dinner and even drink wine. Her smallpox vaccination did not take well, so she had varioloid several times. She also had great difficulty in getting used to the douche room, and fell on the slippery floor several times each year. But it was her pregnancy and deliverance that furnished the best copy. She read so many detailed reports of her own condition that she was enabled to attend his obstetric cases when her husband was engaged elsewhere. With his help she wrote *Water Cure for Ladies*, a combination volume on cooking according to Graham, baby cleansing and feminine beautification.

Dr. Shew's practice and the whole course of water cure in America changed after he was summoned to the basement of 417 Houston Street to attend little Aron Potter who had been taken with the flux. As he walked the two blocks down the Bowery, Dr. Shew could not have expected much from the call. Aron's mother, though worthy and industrious, happened to be the colored cook at Professor Ives' Select Institute for Young Ladies.

At the very time Dr. Shew in the basement was dipping the small black bottom of Aron in a wash tub, on an upper floor Dr. Crane from Leroy Street was treating the professor for gout by sewing him up in several thicknesses of flannel nightshirts. Aron got well in three days; but Professor Ives got worse. Even through the flannels he caught cold and inflammatory rheumatism complicated the gout. The rheumatism finally crept up to his heart and his limbs began to swell until they resembled the legs of Barnum's elephant.

In the meanwhile the cook told Mrs. Ives about Aron's miraculous recovery, and Mrs. Ives told her husband. When Dr. Crane arrived on his next visit Professor Ives was worse, his fever had gone up and his breathing was alarming. How about that water treatment this young doctor from Bond Street had used on Aron, he asked Dr. Crane. Wouldn't that perhaps reduce his own fever and give him enough comfort for at least one night's good sleep?

The water cure was a lot of foolishness, Dr. Crane assured him, just imagination. But if Professor Ives was dissatisfied with his treatment he would call in a specialist from New York University. This gentleman also turned down the water cure, but he did let some blood out of the harassed professor. He and Dr. Crane continued to come to 417 Houston Street several times a day; and the patient still got worse. Finally one night he became delirious and both doctors agreed that only by a miracle could he live till morning.

They summoned his best friends, as was customary, to be with him in his last moments. Among them were the Reverend William Henry Channing, Mr. Osborne MacDaniel and Mr. Parke Benjamin. As the gentlemen sat solemnly near the bedside listening to the professor's labored breathing and his occasional frenzied ravings, Mrs. Ives decided to take matters into her own hands. She slipped down to the basement and told Aron to run for Dr. Shew.

Dr. Shew arrived as quickly as his short thick legs could sprint the distance, and burst dramatically into the room. "If you cure that man," Mrs. Ives kept repeating in a loud voice, "you will never be forgotten." The sorrowful watchers nodded in agreement. Dr. Shew went to work immediately for he realized that within a few minutes the patient would be too far gone for any treatment. He threw off the feather bed and the blankets and tried to pull off those flannel shirts in which the professor had been incased for weeks. But the swelling of his body had made these so tight that they stuck to him like a second skin. So calling for a carving knife, Dr. Shew ripped them to shreds.

In the meanwhile, boiling water had been brought up from the basement, because Professor Ives' condition was so extreme that Dr. Shew was afraid to submit him to the more powerful cold water right away. He plunged several large towels into the steaming pots and flung them, still dripping, upon the patient's body. As he did so a "most loathsome stench filled the room." It was as much as even hearty Dr. Shew could bear without fainting. The odor was indeed so overpowering that Mr. Benjamin, the Reverend Mr. Channing, Mrs. Ives and the attending physicians had to withdraw. But Mr. MacDaniel was of sterner stuff. He stood by and assisted Dr. Shew while he gave the professor a thorough cleansing and got him into a wet sheet. The impact brought the patient to consciousness. By the time the watchers returned he had fallen asleep. Three days later he was on his feet again, and within two weeks was walking about the city.

As Mrs. Ives predicted, Dr. Shew was not forgotten. Had she selected them for the purpose of making him remembered she could not have picked a better trio than the Reverend Mr. Channing, Mr. Benjamin and Mr. MacDaniel.

The Reverend Mr. Channing had for several years been the leader of a group in New York City which sought a "higher and wiser holiness" than that vouchsafed by orthodox Christianity. Mr. MacDaniel was literary assistant to Albert Brisbane, and now that his employer was busy working Fourier's scattered writings into a system of world reform, he was writing the column in the *Tribune* and most of the other articles to which the Brisbane name was signed. Parke Benjamin besides being an experienced writer had been literary editor of most of the influential magazines of the times. All three gentlemen were heavy contributors to that stirring new journal of social progress, the *Harbinger*, which was published by the Brook Farm Phalanx and issued each Saturday morning simultaneously in Boston and New York. They were in a position to spread the doctrine of water cure and they did.

Within a few days the Reverend Mr. Channing left New York and his band of holiness seekers to join the association at West Roxbury. There he described to the transcendentalists the miracle of Professor Ives' recovery. His enthusiasm, backed up by Messrs. MacDaniel's and Benjamin's written testimonials, so impressed the Brook Farmers that the *Harbinger* pronounced editorially that anyone who believed in social progress *must* support the water cure.

This tribute from the highest brows in the country added greatly to Dr. Shew's prestige and to the number and quality of his patients. Naturally it pleased him enormously, but it served only to irritate Colonel James Watson Webb, the cantankerous editor of the *New York Courier and Enquirer*.

Next to his irascible temper which had got him into several duels and once landed him in Sing Sing, Colonel Webb was most noted for getting the news quicker than anybody. He beat not only those upstarts, Greeley, Bennett and W. C. Bryant with their miserable penny

sheets, but even the *Journal of Commerce,* his one rival
in the six-penny field. Back in the thirties when intelligence by stage took almost as many weeks as it now did
hours by the magnetic telegraph, he maintained his own
pony express to Washington. Although steam had cut
the distance from Liverpool to New York to fifteen
days, he still sent his swift schooners a hundred miles
out to sea to meet incoming vessels and get the latest
news from Europe. And now he had been scooped on
the water cure business by a miserable weekly got out
by a lot of crack-pot abolitionists. Though the *Harbinger* carried the most elevating thoughts of Brisbane,
Emerson, Dana and Thoreau concerning all the many
subjects that fired them, to Webb, whose first interest
was politics, it was nothing but an abolitionist mouthpiece. As a good free-soiler Whig, he despised abolitionists more than he did democrats.

Colonel Webb's humiliation was made worse by the
circumstance that at the very same time Professor Ives
was being wrapped in the wet sheet up on Houston
Street, the great Bulwer was undergoing a similar treatment at Malvern, England. Bulwer was so exhilarated
by the experience that he wrote an open letter to the
English press describing the wet sheet as a "magical and
very luxurious remedy—in which pain is lulled, fever
cooled and watchfulness wrapped in slumber." Colonel
Webb had had the first copy of the letter to reach
America, yet he hadn't considered the fact that Bulwer
had taken a bath sufficiently important to be played up

in his paper. The Colonel was now faced with the problem of discovering the water cure several months after it had become famous. It was a cold that he contracted while paying his customary calls on New Year's Day that gave him the solution.

Editor Webb had two guiding rules: get the news while it is hot and make it personal. Though this time he had missed the first, his cold allowed him to apply the second. Coughing and sneezing he presented himself, and his wife and children, at 47 Bond Street and asked Dr. Shew to go to work on them. Appreciating the full publicity value of his visitation, Dr. Shew put the Webbs into wet sheets not just once but three times daily. Within a week the Colonel could lay before his readers Bulwer's four-months-old letter in a truly arresting manner, by comparing his own experiences in the sheet with the famous Englishman's. He agreed about the luxuriousness of the remedy. He predicted that water cure would be universally accepted as the most important branch of medicine. He urged all sufferers to familiarize themselves with its blessings, and recommended to all his readers, no matter where they lived or what the state of their health, the free use of water.

This added boost assured the popularity of water cure. Hydropathic establishments sprang up all over New York, throughout New England, and as far south as Milledgeville, Georgia, and Biloxi, Mississippi. The most elegant were the Orange Mountain Resort, in East

Orange, New Jersey, and Dr. Shew's summer place at Oyster Bay which catered to the Long Island crowd. The most exotic was the forty-patient institution erected especially for the purpose at Northampton, Massachusetts, by Mr. D. Ruggles, a man of color with peculiar qualifications. Dr. Shew recommended this establishment to those he could not accommodate himself because Mr. Ruggles was blind and therefore able to make especially accurate diagnosis by touching his victims' skins.

Within three years after Professor Ives virtually arose from the dead, Dr. Shew could boast of a list of those he had inducted into the mysteries of the wet sheet and the wet girdle that compared not unfavorably with Priessnitz's earls and dukes and Russian princes. Among planters from Virginia and South Carolina, manufacturers from Connecticut, ministers from Massachusetts, popped out such names as President Eliphalet Nott of Union College, Mr. Calvert of Baltimore, Mr. Biddle of Philadelphia, Mrs. L. Mott of Albany, Mr. J. R. Lowell of Massachusetts, Professor H. W. Longfellow of Cambridge, Professor C. E. Stowe and wife Harriet of Cincinnati, Miss Catherine Beecher of East Hampton, and J. Fenimore Cooper of Cooperstown.

V

Malign Influences Versus *Benign Thoughts*

THE THOUGHT OF BEING IN THE SAME ESTABLISHMENT AND SITTING IN THE SAME SITZ BATHS WHERE so many illustrious folk had been and sat was an exalting idea to Mrs. Gove—but one that was over-tinged with worry. From the outward seeming of the Shew place she divined that it must be even more expensive than the establishment at Brattleboro. And $13 was all the money she had in the world. On top of that, both she and Elma needed new clothes. Those that had been soaked in the rain two nights before were the best they had and there had been no room for any more in the trunk, crammed as it was with the books of science and the paraphernalia that no true believer in water cure ever traveled without—four thick linen sheets, six coarse towels, three blankets, the feather bed and the injection instrument.

Mrs. Gove at twilight was sitting before the cozy fire in their pretty room, trying to break the news to Elma that tomorrow they would have to seek cheaper quarters, when Mrs. Shew, followed by the nurse, came

into the room. Maggie was dripping with wet towels
and her mistress carried the baby wrapped in its blanket.
"I bathe him myself every night and morning," she
said. "And you shall see me do it, just as I have described in my Manual."

As the baby bawled against the chill of the towels,
his mother announced happily that though most residents paid $12 a piece for such accommodations, she
had persuaded her husband to let Mrs. Gove and Elma
have this room for $6.00 for the two of them. Further-
more, Mrs. Shew added, Mrs. Gove wasn't to worry
about paying for her board—just stay on as long as was
needful to observe the doctor's practice, or until she
heard from Mr. Godey in Philadelphia about her stories
or from Mayor Harper about publishing her lectures.
To push her luck to the limit Mrs. Gove asked her
hostess' advice about acquiring two new costumes for
$13.

Why, yes, Mrs. Shew said, the shops downtown were
showing some very nice mousseline de laine for 37 cents
the yard. And seventeen yards, if properly cut, should
be enough for dresses for the two of them. And didn't
Mrs. Gove think that a leaf shade of green would go
well with their fair hair, with perhaps bands of white
linen at the neck and on the sleeves for contrast? But
dressmakers, that was the trouble. They were very dear
in New York now; so indeed were laundresses. Just
imagine having to pay a dollar the dozen for the light-

[51]

est underthings! And it cost $5.00 to have the simplest dress made up.

Mrs. Gove was crestfallen, but Mrs. Shew had an idea. Why not buy the material and take it to her dress-maker to have her cut and fit it? She would surely not charge more than a dollar a piece for that. Then Mrs. Gove and Elma could do the stitching, themselves, and the total cost of the finished dresses would be no more than a seamstress would charge for making them.

Enough about clothes and money, Mrs. Shew laughed. There were more pleasant things to contemplate. "I will," she said, "give you a formal introduction to my dreamer."

Mrs. Gove smiled as if she had just been named in Mr. Astor's will, for all during dinner she had observed a dark, philosophic-looking young man turning his doves eyes of brightest jet continually in her direction. Could this, she asked eagerly, be the dreamer to whom Mrs. Shew referred?

Indeed, and more than that, Mrs. Shew explained. He was the most interesting of all her "characters," her fond name for her husband's patients. He was Edgeworth Lazarus, member of the wealthiest Jewish family in New York, who had just been graduated from medical school. His own fine house was just down the block, but he preferred to live at the Water Cure in order to add hydropathy to his other accomplishments. These were so numerous, and his phraseology so odd, that Mrs. Shew could scarce understand a word he said.

Malign Influences Vs. Benign Thoughts

As the two ladies entered the parlor, the young man rose gracefully from his chair. Putting his long black hair out of his dreamy eyes, he said to Mrs. Gove, "I am most happy to make your acquaintance. I flatter myself that we may have affinity."

Mrs. Gove was slightly taken aback. She had already noted that manners in New York were considerably looser than in New England, but she thought she had met the ultimate in male overtures in the chatelaine approach. That was when a gentleman upon being introduced to a lady bowed low, stared at her girdle, and exclaimed, "May I beg leave to examine your chatelaine?" The subsequent dallying with the various dangling trinkets was the excuse for a prolonged tête-à-tête—or occasionally, perchance, a pinch on the behind.

Mrs. Shew noticing that the abrupt mention of affinities had left Mrs. Gove temporarily speechless, came tactfully to the rescue. "La," said she, "my dreamer means you no hurt. But just now he is over head and ears in Mr. Brisbane's associationism and talks about attractional harmony and passional hygiene and ever so many other words that not nine persons from a hundred can define."

"I believe, Madame," said the intense young man, his eyes glittering like the Koh-i-noor and with the force and feeling of a true prophet in his voice, "that it is only by discriminative attainment of those natural affinities toward which the passional fountain of our life eternally wells up, that life becomes divine, and we escape passional blasphemy."

Mrs. Shew looked aslant at Mrs. Gove with the utmost archness—the expression that most of the young men at the Water Cure found irresistible but which caused the more serious among her husband's acquaintances to declare that she had not a brain in her head. But Mrs. Gove nodded musingly. She had caught in the fine phrases an elusive resemblance to the transcendental conversations of Channing, Alcott and Emerson, and knew the expected rejoinder. "Spoken like a true philosopher," she said patly.

This pleased the young man so much that he begged that she accompany him the next evening to the Park Theater.

"And have you really got Mr. Booth so that he can play Pescara without getting so drunk as to drown all the words in the part?" Mrs. Shew asked skeptically.

"He *lives* the character now, Madame," Dr. Lazarus replied with dignity, "and you hear his words because his life is extended into them."

He then explained to Mrs. Gove that until recently Junius Brutus Booth had been one of the most progressive of thinkers. For a dozen years he had always consulted the great phrenologist Orson Fowler before selecting his roles. And he had conscientiously followed the water cure. Yet in spite of this he had lately become subject to that species of madness known as "subversive charm." His physician had prescribed magnetism as the only treatment which combined the physical and spiritual influences necessary to counterpoise the outraged passions of his darkened soul. But so far gone was the actor in his malady that he knowingly and of his full consent was drawn down the road opposite to that he aimed at, and resisted the magnetic force.

His friends decided that since his physician could not get to him on the spiritual plane, they would have to take hold of his will by the organic end; and influence his subjective proclivities by modifying his external environment.

The most baneful of these environmental forces seemed to emanate from somewhere within the Park Theater during his playing of Pescara. So seven of his friends, Dr. Lazarus among them, sat in front row seats at every performance, seeking to counterpoise the malign influence with their own benign thoughts. But during the first three evenings Booth mumbled and stumbled about the stage worse than ever. He acted, as several persons remarked, like a drunken Irishman.

This observation gave his well-wishers a new idea. The source of the evil influence was undoubtedly the pit of the Park, crowded as it always was with the uncouth b-hoys from the Bowery and their buxom servant girl companions, holding every one of them hateful thoughts against the English. After this the counter-thinkers sat in the pit. By the seventh evening they had things so well controlled that Booth went through his part without falling down.

The next evening Mrs. Gove and Elma, accompanied by Dr. Lazarus and his sister Elena, were witnesses to the recovery. Since on this occasion Mary Gove added her own strong magnetic powers to those of Booth's other well-wishers, the great actor gave an especially moving performance.

After the play the little girls were taken to the American Museum. The mother and brother smiled indulgently at their awe of the exhibits, for they appreciated Mr. Barnum's effort, through his whale and mermaid, to interest the general in science. But just around the corner, at the intersection of Nassau and Beecham Streets was a museum far more wonderful to sophisticated folk like themselves.

Old Clinton Hall, originally built on land donated by Philip Hone as the home of New York's first public library, now housed the more famous and informative Phrenological Cabinet. Though it was now being pushed hard by less austere disciplines, phrenology was still the most firmly established of the modern sciences. It had been taught in America by Gall's only collaborator and the heir to all his lore, John Gaspar Spurzheim. To progressives like Mrs. Gove and Dr. Lazarus the story of the great man's tragic visit to our country was the most inspiring episode in our cultural history.

He had come over in the spring of 1832 to deliver a series of lectures in New York; and found another European visitor, unexpected and unwanted, here before him. Cholera, brought across the Atlantic for the first time in history by a boatload of Irish immigrants, had struck New York. Its victims were dying by the hundreds every day.

More than half the population, all that could afford it, had fled the city—to Murray Hill, Harlem Heights and Long Island. The stock exchange and the mercantile establishments were closed. Only the churches were allowed to remain open—to hold special prayers for the stricken. All other public gatherings were forbidden. Spurzheim, under the protective wing of Professor Amariah Brigham, anatomist of Columbia, was hurried off to the healthier climate of Connecticut.

It was propitious for the intellectual life of America that he was. Had he given his demonstrations in New York and then returned to Paris, he might have been remembered as just another in the series of glamorous foreigners who were discovering in New York the best show town in the world. Compared to Dickens, the actor MacCready, the non-interventionist Louis Kossuth, to say nothing of the three incomparable Fannies—Miss Wright the lecturer, Miss Kemble the actress, and Miss Essler the dancer—he might even have seemed dull. But New England found in him that oft fulfilled dream of the intellectuals—a master scientist and a god.

VI

John Gaspar Spurzheim Brings Phrenology to America

SPURZHEIM ARRIVED IN NEW HAVEN DURING COMMENCEMENT WEEK AT YALE. HE WAS GREETED BY THE college's three most imposing figures, President Day, Governor Trumball and Professor Silliman, who was America's most noted natural scientist. They hastily added his name to the list of Commencement Day speakers.

He not only spoke but dissected the brain of a child recently dead of dropsy of the brain. With equal adroitness he analyzed the characters of an assorted group of living men, distinguished alumni back for commencement, augmented by contingents from the Asylum for the Deaf and Dumb, the Retreat for the Insane and the State Prison. Not once while he ran his large sensitive hands over their crania did he confuse the criminals with the mutes, or the lunatics with the alumni.

The Yale faculty, in love of him, as Silliman expressed it, formed a phrenological society for the purpose of perpetuating his science among their students. News of this honor went on before him as the great man proceeded to Boston to repeat his performance at Harvard's graduating festivities.

The notables of that institution who waited upon him included President Quincy, Judge Storey and Professor Nathaniel Bowditch, Harvard's entrant as challenger to Silliman's title as America's foremost scientist. The performances at Harvard on Commencement Day, and the next evening before the Society of Phi Beta Kappa, were so impressive that the Medical Faculty persuaded him to give them a special course of instruction. And the most cultured citizens of Boston, ministers, physicians, school proprietors and society matrons, induced him to cross the Charles in the evenings for a series of popular lectures. The Boston Atheneum gave way to the more spacious Masonic Temple, which in turn yielded to the legislative hall of the State House, in the increasing rush of ticket buyers.

Yet the series of eighteen lectures was never completed, for the constitution that had warded off Asiatic cholera fell ingloriously under the assaults of New England victualry. Believing in no science but his own the great man had to become unconscious before outside help could be called in. The ministrations of Dr. James Jackson, Harvard's famed professor of the Theory and Practice of Physic, proved unavailing; and three months after his arrival in America, his bedroom packed with admirers with ears bent for an illuminating last word, the soul of John Gaspar Spurzheim departed from these shores. His body, however, prolonged the visit.

The funeral procession which followed it from the Old South Meeting House, where the first and more exclusive obsequies were held, to the more commodious Park Street Church, where an encore for the public was given, was the most "exciting" ever assembled in Massachusetts. Behind the sorrowing President Quincy walked Dean John Warren and Harvard's entire Medical Faculty, President Winslow Lewis and the Boston Medical Society, municipal and state dignitaries, and notables from the cultural institutions of Connecticut. The eulogies were delivered by the leading ministers of Boston, aided by the more oratorical schoolmasters and Harvard's professors of elocution.

Professor Follen declared, "The Prophet is gone but his Mantle is upon us." To which Horace Mann, superintendent of schools for Massachusetts, added that phrenology was the truest handmaiden of Christianity. The Reverend Mr. John Pierpont, famed as a hymnologist, began to send—and rhythmically beat out the Austrian with the Godhead. Hosea Ballou, Edward Beecher, Joseph Tuckermann, Father Taylor, Ellery Channing, and the other priests and ministers who preached his successive funerals seemed likewise to confuse the co-founder of phrenology with the Founder of Christianity.

As soon as the apotheosized body was stored in its vault, all these notables, with President Quincy, Professor Bowditch, Dr. William Alcott, Dr. Samuel Howe and more than a hundred of the most distinguished physicians, lawyers, clergymen, artists, professors and merchants of Boston, returned to the deceased's late apartments to decide how his memory could be best served. By unanimous approval President Quincy appointed Drs. Jackson and Lewis to excise the Spurzheim brain and heart and to separate his skull from the rest of him.

These cuts, properly preserved, were put on exhibition at various places around the Harvard Yard while the more literary members of the committee sent letters to scientific societies in Paris, London, Dublin and Edinburgh, soliciting bids for the various sections of the great man. When these letters had gone unanswered for a year it began to be apparent that Europe wanted no part of him.

The carcass, ill-equipped for that glorious resurrection morn mentioned in the eulogies, was placed beneath a handsome marble, the first ever erected in Mt. Auburn Cemetery, and thus hallowed the ground later to be enriched by Channings, Fullers, Emersons, Warrens, Ballous, etc. The other organs stayed on at Harvard to bedevil its officials until this day. And a strange uneasiness began to pervade the 144 members of the Boston Phrenological Society. This became a stronger emotion when the next issue of the *Princeton Review* appeared.

The professors at the New Jersey college had been understandably peeved when Spurzheim's sponsors in New York, in order to get him away from the cholera, had routed him up the Sound instead of across the Hudson. They would have liked to ignore his triumphs in Connecticut and Massachusetts, but the Boston papers would not let them.

They read that so great was the esteem in which Spurzheim was held that often he had to attend divine services five times on a single Sabbath in order to occupy all the pews in which he was invited to sit—to drag a distinguished visitor off to church seemed hospitable to good Bostonians and more of an honor than an invitation to dinner. For all his church-going and for all the detailed reports of his many lectures the Princetonians noted one glaring omission: Spurzheim had not once even mentioned the After Life. Silence on such a topic might indeed be seemly to Unitarians but to the disgruntled Presbyterians it might prove a key to the man's real character.

So the dons of Princeton did what in the excitement of heaping honors the professors at Yale and Harvard had not thought to do. They rooted up back numbers of foreign magazines and inquired into Spurzheim's past. Their search was rewarding.

Spurzheim and Gall had been expelled from their native Vienna in 1802 by a special order of the Austrian Government which declared their teachings to be dangerous to religion and morality. Prussia, then laved by the mysticism of Kant and Goethe, construed this declaration a recommendation, and for five years the Austrian émigrés did a thriving business in Berlin, lecturing to the scientists and demonstrating upon the prisoners.

Paris, lush with the first fruits of Empire, beckoned, and for a few fleeting weeks Gall and Spurzheim were the sensation of the city. They frankly bid the ladies of the court to have their "fortunes told by their heads." But when they asked permission to settle permanently, Napoleon referred them to Cuvier, head of the new French Institute.

The great zoologist, surrounded by his colleagues, let the Austrians present their case. Then he demonstrated to the Institute that if the phrenologists were correct about the location and relative size of the thinking organs and those appropriate to man, then mice, moles, sheep and goats would be wiser than the most learned human who ever lived, and turtles, sharks, frogs and canary birds almost twice as brilliant. The Institute sent Gall and Spurzheim packing as fast as thirty years before the Royal Academy, under Lavoisier and Franklin, had sent another refugee from Austria, Anton Mesmer.

Gall and Spurzheim were at first undismayed. Their expulsion from Paris, they believed, would make them as welcome in London as being thrown out of Vienna had enhanced their reputation in Berlin. But London scientists had read the French Institute's report, and so had those in Dublin and Edinburgh. Sir Charles Bell, the great anatomist, declared phrenology to be "the most extravagant departure from all legitimate modes of reasoning that I have ever encountered."

The pair went back to examining the prisoners in Berlin, where they stayed until the return of the Bourbons made fortune telling profitable for a brief time in Paris. There Gall died in 1827 in the comparative obscurity from which the invitation to America saved Spurzheim.

The *Princeton Review* published these findings in detail; the *North American* and the *American Quarterly* dutifully reprinted them. To make matters the more embarrassing the rumor got about in Cambridge that Dean Warren of the Medical School claimed to have known all along that Spurzheim was a fraud. All the other professors at both Harvard and Yale rallied around Presidents Quincy and Day in preserving the reputation of the great man as well as they had his various organs. But their students thought the whole affair amusing, and the Hasty Pudding Club in honor of Dean Warren, a charter member, made bawdy ridicule of bump-feeling.

To get in on the fun, Amherst College, which had the snappiest debating society in the East, decided to stage a public debate on "Is Phrenology a Science?" at which the paid customers would act as judges. To assure the audience the "infinite in merriment" as well as instruction, Henry Ward Beecher, the wittiest student, was chosen as negative deponent.

Although the debate was announced far ahead

Beecher, out of respect to his brilliance, postponed boning up on the subject until two days before the event. Then he found that the material in the Amherst library was woefully meager. The reprinted stuff in the American reviews was almost twenty years old, and besides, the boys at Harvard and Yale had already squeezed it dry. To be original he sent to Boston for the latest works on the subject.

The stage service was disrupted on account of early snow, the books delayed, and the debate postponed for two weeks. During that time Beecher studied every page of his new volumes. When he arose to convince the "cream of the neighboring townships" that phrenology was not a science he surpassed himself. The audience rocked with laughter and with hardly a dissenting voice voted phrenology a fraud.

Then to their amazement young Beecher stepped to the front of the platform and asked their indulgence a while longer. Now without humor but in deadly earnest he took up the arguments that he himself had used against phrenology and demolished them one by one. The cream of the neighborhood quickly changed to soft butter under his eloquent ministrations and agreed unanimously that phrenology was a science. They cheered young Beecher lustily and told one another, "That young fellow is a real orator. Already he speaks better than his father and his brother."

Before he could leave the rostrum his dearest friend leaped nimbly up to embrace him. It was almost too

much for the flushed orator. "Fowler," he said in that
tone which so many thousands were to find irresistible,
"let's retire to a quiet place." And Orson Squire Fowler, who had adored Henry Ward Beecher since they
started school together, followed his idol to his room.

On the threshold Fowler shuddered at the sight
which still shocked him after six years of friendship—
the amazing disorder of Beecher's room. The phrenological works were scattered from floor to the window-
sill in a jumble of soiled towels and underclothes.
Hastily rooting out a volume Fowler discovered from
its illustrative chart the location of the faculty of Order.
Then, following the "Practical Directions to Practi-
tioners," he placed the first knuckle of his second finger
gingerly on his friend's head.

To his surprise and delight he found that Beecher's
organ of order was "almost wholly wanting." And to
his subject's delight, if not entirely to his surprise, he
found that the Beecher bumps of Power of Thought,
Cogency of Argument, Clearness of Illustration, Eloquence, and Splendor of Diction, as well as those for
Benevolence, Humor, and Sense of Character, were
larger than any illustrated in the charts.

That settled for Beecher the idea that had struck him
that evening during the bursts of applause. Despite his
love of merriment, he would follow the family tradition and become a preacher, but certainly the most eloquent, splendid, cogent, humorous and benevolent of
them all. Even after he became all of this to his wor-

shipers, he never forgot this crisis in his life. At least three times a year he would retell it to his congregation at Plymouth Church.

Under the spell of his tremendous bump for Clearness of Illustration he would wind up, "And were I the owner of an island in mid-ocean, and had all books, apparatus and appliances, tools to cultivate the soil, manufacture, cook, and carry on life's affairs in comfort and refinement, and some dark night pirates should come and burn my books, musical instruments, works of art, furniture, tools, and machinery, and leave me the land and the empty barns and house, I should be, in respect to the successful carrying on of my affairs, in very much the same plight that I should be as a preacher if Phrenology and all that it has taught me of man, his character, his wants and improvement, were blotted from my mind."

If phrenology set Beecher to his calling, it did even more for Fowler. He stayed up all night memorizing charts, and the very next day began to explore the heads of his fellow students. His admiration and delight grew with each experiment as he discovered "ever more perfect coincidences between his friends' phrenological developments and what he knew of their characters."

One who was slow at figures had a very small organ of Calculation; another who excelled at map-making had Locality very large; and two boys who were notorious throughout the college for their egotism and self-conceit were discovered to have the organs of Self-Esteem in such a degree as to elongate their heads. Dr. Humphrey, the venerable president of Amherst, who was pre-eminent as a divine and a metaphysician, had the requisite bumps, too.

Upon his graduation the following June Orson Fowler persuaded his father to finance him to a year's phrenological tour, and to allow his brother Lorenzo to quit the Academy and become his assistant. The two ambitious young men set out through New England and New York State, giving lectures and public demonstrations in town halls, schools and meeting houses; holding private consultations at their boarding houses; diagnosing patients for the keepers of lunatic asylums; warning parents of signs of Destructiveness and Combativeness in their offsprings' crania; advising aging spinsters about making themselves more attractive to possible suitors; and helping housewives to select honest and respectable servant girls. They left satisfied customers in every village through which they passed.

VII

Exploring the Craniums of the Great

THE FOWLER BROTHERS BEGAN TO GET OFF THE BORSCHT CIRCUIT AND HEAD TOWARD THE BIG TIME when they hit Troy. The attention they received there, however, was a tribute not so much to their own talents as to the cultural acumen of Mrs. Emma Willard, headmistress of the Female Academy.

When some fifteen years earlier she set out to prove that young ladies could become as well educated as young gentlemen without losing one whit of their charm and modesty, Mrs. Willard had written a sharp note to DeWitt Clinton, informing him that it was his duty as Governor of New York to supply her with state-paid male teachers of science. Though by 1825 her Troy Female Academy had grown so famous that Lafayette visited it, Clinton's successors in Albany had continued to ignore the memorial letter she addressed to them each year. She seized on the Fowlers as a means of acquainting her young ladies with the most useful of the sciences in a manner that would prove to the Governors how practical were her demands. On the phrenologists' second night in the city the young ladies tripped to the stage of the town hall while the male citizenry gawked.

Orson Fowler did not disappoint their headmistress. By such skillful manipulations that he did not disturb a hair-do he pointed out which of them were proficient at their painting lessons, which excelled in the embroidery classes; as well as those in whom Hope was so deficient as to make them shy in the presence of strange men, and those in whom Approbativeness was so strong as to render them bold. Of one miss who fitted snugly into the latter category he said further that her Ideality, Comparison and Language were so large that she not only read poetry appreciatively but was able to compose it.

A titter followed this announcement, for everyone knew that Emmaline never opened a book outside of the classroom and hardly had a thought above filling her stomach. Yet a few months later she wrote Mr. Fowler that she had composed enough verses to fill a volume and where, please, should she send them for publication?

Stopping in New York City long enough to examine young P. T. Barnum's latest importation, the Siamese Twins, and announce dramatically that Eng and Chan actually had two brains, the Fowlers headed for Pennsylvania. The publicity they had got from Mrs. Willard and the amazement they had evoked over their diagnosis of the Siamese gave them full bookings. They were also invited to dinner parties and soirées where they conscientiously fingered the heads of their hosts. It was in Philadelphia that something really wonderful happened to them. They were summoned by Mr. Nicholas Biddle to his office at the Bank of the United States.

Visitors to the Bank had been few since Jackson had withdrawn the Government's credit three years before. And the Fowler boys might well have expected to find an ogre awaiting them there, for the reform press was still yelling for Biddle to be put in jail, declaring that his greed and cupidity had drawn enough tears from cheated widows and impoverished orphans to float the Savannah from New York to Liverpool. But it was not of his own troubles or the financial condition of the country that Mr. Biddle wished to talk. In his private safe he rummaged through stocks and bonds, recently worth thousands of dollars, and brought out an object carefully wrapped in velvet. Before unwrapping it he told the brothers a little story.

In the summer of 1806, before assuming his duties as secretary to Minister Monroe in London, Nicholas Biddle had taken a short pleasure jaunt on the Continent. In an inn in Karlsruhe he had struck up an acquaintance with a talented young man from Austria named Francis Gall. Besides his regular luggage Dr. Gall had with him seven heavy plaster busts upon which he was continually drawing diagrams. The busts represented the heads of six Austrian generals and Napoleon Bonaparte. From his calculations, Gall confided to his fellow guest, he had made sure that Napoleon would win at Austerlitz. Biddle was so impressed that he had a cast of his own head made and asked Gall to foretell his future. He reverently unveiled the cast and showed it to the Fowlers.

The brothers were tongue-tied with awe. But after they left, a tremendous thought occurred to them. On Mr. Biddle's cast there had been a huge blank space where modern phrenologists now placed, among several others, the organ of Conscientiousness—apparently because in 1806 Gall had not yet perfected his system and located all the organs. Yet that blank space contained the answer to the question which had been agitating the American electorate for four years.

If the Biddle bump of Conscientiousness was small then he was, as the Democrats said, a scoundrel and a robber of orphans. But if his Conscientiousness was large, then he was as honest as Mr. Monroe had thought when he was persuaded by Biddle to re-charter his father's Bank; and not his mismanagement, but President Jackson's cunning, had caused the Bank's fall.

Nelson Fowler, being younger and more impetuous than his brother, thought they should go back and settle the question right then. But Orson, though respecting the opinions of reform editors like William Cullen Bryant and Henry Raymond as much as the facts of science, said the experience would certainly be unpleasant. Even if by some miracle an examination should vindicate Mr. Biddle, it would do little practical good;

it couldn't restore the lost fortunes of the widows and orphans. The rulers of the nation's future were not in Philadelphia but some hundred miles farther to the south. And wouldn't it be wonderful if they could examine America's rulers and reveal to the country what manner of men they really were?

It was a heady idea to come to two young men whose own bumps of Hope were extraordinarily large. They took the steam cars for Washington.

When they crossed the Ellicott River they well knew that they were entering enemy territory. Baltimore had outlawed phrenology, even before the *North American* and the *Princeton Review* had printed the French and Scotch disparagements of Spurzheim and Gall, when George Henry Calvert had tried to introduce it there.

This great grandson of Lord Baltimore had, like Nicholas Biddle, enjoyed the broadening influence of European travel. He had stayed with Goethe at Weimar and become acquainted with Gall after his phrenological system was perfected. When upon his return to Baltimore in the late 1820's Mr. Calvert told the proprietors of the book shops that he would give free instruction in phrenology to all the pupils they sent him, the physicians of the town had ganged up on their most eminent citizen and informed the public that Gall was a fraud. The book sellers stopped circulating Mr. Calvert's offer and that gentleman soon afterwards quit his native town forever to settle in the more congenial spiritual climate of Newport, Rhode Island.

The Mad Forties

On the Virginia side of Washington, at Alexandria, stood the Episcopal Theological Seminary which controlled the spiritual destiny of the South. There Dean Ruel Keith was teaching his students, and instructing them to impress on their future congregations, that the "pretensions of phrenology are not only false, but very prejudicial to the interests of morality and religion." Within the capital itself was John Quincy Adams who had frequently sworn, even while Spurzheim was being glutted toward his dismemberment, that he didn't see how one phrenologist could look at another without breaking into loud guffaws.

Into this hostile environment the Fowlers came unafraid, and prepared to stay until the biggest heads in the land bowed to their monkey-like gropings. In Washington they were fortunate in sharing floor space with a man of peculiar talents.

John Henri Browere, a neighbor and friend of the Fowler family on Roosevelt Street in New York, was the most noted cast-maker in America. His ambition was to create a portrait gallery of the outstanding personages of his day. He had done Lafayette, Thomas Jefferson, Alexander Hamilton, Dolly Madison, DeWitt Clinton, Dr. Valentine Mott and Colonel William Leete Stone. The Fowlers later tried to give the impression that it was he who joined them in Washington in casting the same heads they were examining. It was not the old man but his son. Young Browere, however, was the possessor of his father's secret for making the casts; a secret that was buried with him.

Among their first customers in the capital was Junius Brutus Booth, who walked in holding the hand of his youngest son. Orson Fowler advised him that a man of his magnificent phrenological development could be at home only in the noblest roles.

The departing Booths were brusquely pushed aside by an energetic gentleman with a Tidewater accent, who refused to give his name unless his examination proved satisfactory. Orson Fowler reassured him right away that he was possessed of a towering ambition, a propelling intellect, and a unique combination of Combativeness and Destructiveness that augured an unrivaled talent for cutting and withering sarcasms.

As everybody in Washington knew that John Quincy Adams and Henry Wise cut and withered each other every day in the lesser hall of Congress, and as the visitor did not talk Back Bay, it comes as no surprise that he was indeed the latter. Representative Wise, who was a Virginia gentleman and contrarily a Jacksonian Democrat, left in a cloud of Pennsylvania Avenue dust as he hastened to the White House to gloat over Adams being proved wrong again.

Reporters from all the Washington and Baltimore papers were present at the first public performance, held in the Unitarian Church, to see the young phrenologist function with his face covered—a necessary precaution since the church was jammed with notables whom he might recognize by sight. When at the end of his lecture he called for volunteers for the demonstration, a group of physicians, who shared the skepticism of their colleagues over in Maryland, rushed forward scoffingly. The groping hands fastened upon a skull which was immediately described as possessed of extraordinary independence joined with great energy and force of character.

The audience gasped. Even the physicians swallowed the birds on their lips and nodded in amazed agreement. The skull so accurately described belonged to Dr. Hunt who just a few days before had refused any longer to serve the Jackson family because the President declined to down his physic. In their stories the next day the Washington journalists echoed the positive headline of the *United States Telegraph*, "Phrenology Vindicated!!!" This paper was the Administration mouthpiece and the property of Duff Green, head of the notorious Kitchen Cabinet and seasoned Adams-baiter.

Andrew Jackson read these stories with interest, and the next day his crony General Green, accompanied by a party of friends, appeared at the Fowler office and demanded a *written* interpretation of his character. This was an unusual request. Ordinarily a chart with the various organs marked very small, small, average, large, very large or extraordinary, was all that the Fowlers gave for their fee. But there was something so important in General Green's manner and such a tense air of excitement in his little group, that the phrenologists decided to comply.

It was well for them and for the future of their science in the United States of America that they did. The character sketch was immediately rushed to the White House where Jackson studied it seriously and pronounced it remarkable. As a result the Fowlers were allowed the supreme privilege of analyzing the First Head in the Land. It was luckily also the largest—as anyone who has ever licked a postage stamp now knows —and the most splendidly equipped they had ever encountered. The Administration forces had scored another victory over the obstructionist Representative from Massachusetts.

With the Jackson chart in their files there was not a bump in Washington that a first knuckle of a second Fowler finger could not caress at will. Happily the organs of the nation's great men, like those of the Amherst students, coincided perfectly with what was known of their characters. Clay's, Calhoun's and Webster's heads were as full of bumps as pre-LaGuardia burlesque.

If the Fowlers had nothing good to tell of a public figure they kept silent. Of the rambunctious Thomas Hart Benton they merely remarked that his head was big and the organs that gave him force immense; of Vice President Johnson they said he was kind to his family. Though they examined Van Buren several times while he was a candidate for President they kept their findings secret until after his retirement, when they declared that his head, like Benton's, Biddle's, Chief Keokuk's and those of thirty other Indian chieftains, showed a temperament that tried to get by without working.

While this reticence evidently kept the examinations from having any marked effect on the 1836 elections (a careful check shows that when it came to the really high class faculties like Marvelousness, Veneration and Ideality, the Whigs had a slight edge on the Democrats), there is no doubt that they convinced the nation of the scientific accuracy of phrenology. In the meanwhile, the lifelike castings of young Browere, each one marked by the phrenological findings of the Fowlers, were growing in number. When they reached above a thousand of the most distinguished men in both church and state, the brothers possessed enough goods to fill the racks of two Phrenological Cabinets; one on Chestnut Street in Philadelphia; the larger and more important in Clinton Hall.

It was in the New York Cabinet that the College of Phrenologists, composed of all the doctors, lawyers, ministers, writers, artists, teachers and merchants, who had temporarily left their more normal occupations to cash in on the Fowlers' fame, had their headquarters and held their meetings. It was there, too, that any resident New Yorker or any visitor to the city with the least claim to being up-to-date went to have his phrenological chart marked by the same hands that had marked his President's.

The Phrenological Cabinet served not only as a gathering place for the College of Phrenologists but as a clearing house for their findings. Whenever one examined a particularly interesting head—of a distinguished personage, an idiot, a lunatic, a notorious criminal or a rare animal, like a tiger or wild cat—he had casts made from the measurements and traded them to his fellow scientists for their equivalent in other striking specimens. The Boston Phrenological Society had a fortunate position in this cranial bargaining, second if not equal to that of the Fowlers.

The Bostonians not only had in Spurzheim's own pickled brain the final reference in any doctrinal dispute, but through the autopsies which Dr. Joseph Jackson performed on the great men who died near Boston or were brought there to be buried, they were able to compare the insides of other powerful brains with the charts that had been made of the famous ones' skulls while they were still alive. The Boston committee were also proprietors of the charts which Dr. Samuel Howe made of the afflicted children at the Blind School, and these were particularly valuable. The cast of the blind mute Laura Bridgman, whom Dr. Howe taught to read, write, talk, recite poetry and take an interest in the finer things of life—in fact to do everything that Helen Keller years later learned to do by the same method—was worth as much in trade as the Fowlers' masks of Booth and Black Hawk, or twice as much as those of Van Buren and Benton.

The Boston committee also possessed in the person of Dr. John Pierpont phrenology's greatest bulwark against those ignorant people who charged that it was an heretical doctrine. Before any newcomer was admitted to the College of Phrenologists, no matter how great his academic attainments, his spiritual soundness had to be attested to by the minister who had discovered in Spurzheim the qualities usually assigned to Deity.

The meetings of the College of Phrenologists were especially enjoyable times for the Reverend Mr. Pierpont because now that he was bereft of a helpmeet they gave him the opportunity to pay discreet court to Orson Fowler's sister. He had just returned from such gallantries when he was waited upon by a sharp-faced, intense little woman who introduced herself as Mrs. Hiram Gove from over in Lynn. She presented him with a glowing letter of recommendation from his close friend and former business associate, John Neal.

VIII
Some Feminine Protégés

JOHN PIERPONT HAD BEEN AN ADVEN-
TURESOME YOUNG BUCK MORE IN-
TERESTED IN WORLDLY WEALTH
than in the riches of the soul when, after graduating
from Yale and serving the customary postgraduate
year as tutor to a planter's family, he persuaded John
Neal to join him in establishing a dry goods store in the
young town of Baltimore. The venture from a material
standpoint was a flop. The youthful partners had just
got settled when the War of 1812 broke out, and then
came the depression which followed the embargo. Moreover, among the unserious folk of Baltimore the two
refugees became lonely for the peculiar culture of their
homeland.

As a protest they made a typically New England
gesture; they founded a literary society and a magazine. The applause which his fellow Delphians gave
the original hymns he recited at their meetings persuaded John Pierpont that perhaps the selling of dry
goods was not the function for which he had been ordained. In 1819 he quit Baltimore and commercialism
to enter the Harvard Divinity School.

The praise which the intelligentsia of London heaped on his homey stories of his native Maine, when rather hesitantly he sent copies of the *Portico* to the great English magazines, decided Neal on an even more daring course. He would go to London and become a literary man. He was an immediate success. In 1825 *Blackwood's* serialized his *Brother Jonathan*, the first novel to give the English a completely satisfactory American hero— earthy, lovable, humorous and shrewd. "Brother Jonathan" was the name that for years afterwards Englishmen applied to America, and its creator became a great favorite in the liberal circles of London. Jeremy Bentham was so delighted with him that he insisted that he live at his house.

It was while staying at the Bentham home, and absorbing the Bentham ideas for reorganizing society, that Neal first met an even more devoted Bentham protégé —Frances Wright, just then flushed with her success of having outwitted Lafayette's relatives by accompanying the General on his triumphant tour of America. From the hour of that meeting John Neal became a profound believer in the unlimited rights of women.

One thing that Neal's English admirers could not understand was why he preferred to live anywhere but in his idyllic America. Catching the nostalgia in his own works he, too, began to wonder why he stayed away. So after four years he came home, intending to settle in New York. But by 1827 New York with the best harbor on the seaboard was becoming cosmopolitan. Neal found there few of the homey customs about which he had written so enthusiastically in London. He left the growing metropolis and settled in Portland at the truly American occupation of a real estate business with a little lawyering on the side.

But his literary reputation, which was surpassed by none and challenged only by Cooper, pursued him there. His opinion was sought by New England magazines on many subjects. He willingly endorsed new ideas and, even more generously, new writers. He encouraged Whittier to write rhymes as well as diatribes against slavery, and was the first critic to recognize the genius of Edgar Allan Poe.

Neal was particularly proud of his influence upon the women of New England. Three whom he inspired to express themselves in writing and upon the lecture platform became famous. A speech he delivered in Providence when she was teaching there was elaborated by Margaret Fuller into *Woman in the Nineteenth Century*. His enthusiasm for Joan of Arc, Madame de Stael and Sappho was caught by Elizabeth Oakes Smith, and enabled her to inject some much needed culture into the proceedings of the Women's Rights Party. But of all his feminine protégés the one of whom John Neal was proudest was his own distant relative, Mary Neal Gove. She was his first and his most idolatrous pupil. She not only wrote and proclaimed his ideas, she lived them.

Her meeting with Neal at the home of mutual relatives in her native New Hampshire was the most exciting thing which up till that time had happened to Mrs. Gove. He was the first person she had ever seen who had traveled into the great world, and she could not understand his devotion to that section of America which, still beguiled by his own writing, he persisted in calling "Sunny New England."

"Sunny it may be to some," Mary Gove retorted, "but it is a hard-favored Fatherland to many, many more." The typical New England village, she reminded him, was an ugly, treeless, desolate, joyless town, built about and dominated by a graveyard, which could have but one possible justification—"to serve as a warning against the erection of another such."

But the thing about John Neal that interested Mary Gove even more than his wide travels and his peculiar taste in towns was the fact that he had been read out of the Society of Friends. At the time she met him she was consumed by a tremendous resentment toward Quakers in general and one Quaker in particular.

At the frightening age of twenty-one, while visiting in a neighboring village, she had met and been diffidently courted by an old bachelor named Hiram Gove. Her first feeling toward him had been one of deep and most decided aversion. Even after several weeks' acquaintance she could find nothing about him to recommend him except his piety, but since she herself was at this time quite pious, also, she thought that would be a sufficient basis for marriage, especially since he practiced his piety in a Friends' Meeting House. She had heard that Quakers allowed their women more freedom than any other sect. Having been reared in submissive Calvinism, she thought it would be wonderful to speak out in meeting among all the men.

Yet her marriage, she confided to Neal, had turned into an abyss of evil which she had no words to describe. It wasn't so much that a convulsive spasm ran over her whole system every time that Hiram approached her or laid a hand upon her, but that he had denied her the very freedoms for which she had married him. Outside of meeting he treated her worse than if he had bought her on the block at the South. He forbade her to read anything but the Bible and obituaries; he stopped her from writing poetry which he called a black art; he said all Methodists were libertines and would not allow her to speak to them; he wouldn't let her out of the house except to go to meeting and to funerals. Why, the Quakers, she told Neal indignantly, were worse than the Calvinists.

In this baffled indignation John Neal recognized fertile soil for sowing the ideas he had picked up from his liberal friends in England. He told Mary Gove that no form of orthodox Christianity offered her any hope. Like that gallant band of English women who had dared follow Mary Wollstonecraft, she must fight for her own freedom against all the forces that now enslaved her—the law, the church, public opinion, and the false interpretation that ignorant men put upon the Scriptures.

This was such exciting news to Mrs. Gove that she announced that she was going to be the Wollstonecraft of America. Though she had but the slightest formal education she would henceforth dedicate herself to teaching her countrywomen what they should know about themselves. It was characteristic of her that having made this decision she did not bother about those niceties of ethics and of social relationships that so often disturbed her model. Instead, she procured a textbook of anatomy and set herself to learning all she could about the female innards.

She had mastered this subject to the astounding discovery of the connection between the foetus and its mother, when her husband moved from the New Hampshire woods to the booming mill town of Lynn. Neal supplied her with letters to his two best friends in the vicinity—Henry Longfellow in Cambridge and John Pierpont in Boston.

Longfellow made little impression on her—after all, she wrote poetry herself. But knowing Pierpont was an experience. Until she met him she was absolutely certain that John Neal was destined to be the most famous writing man of the next two centuries. But now she was not so sure. John Pierpont was that wonderful creature she had not dared believe could exist in this world: a man of God who was excessively pious, yet at the same time completely liberal-minded. Under his benign influence she quickly added phrenology to her growing knowledge.

She had just discovered in her own scalp towering organs of Self-esteem, Combativeness, Amativeness and Sublimity, when John Neal stopped by on his way home from a lecture tour in Rhode Island to report that President Wayland and the faculty of Brown University had pronounced mesmerism a more profound and basic science than phrenology. Neal himself while in Providence had seen evidences of the magnetic influence that were well nigh incredible.

Miss Margaret Fuller when she became filled with it could strike men dumb just by entering a room. Other ladies had discovered within themselves clairvoyant powers a hundred times more wonderful. Mothers were using the magnetic fluid in place of laudanum for pacifying their squalling young. Even little children, having peeped upon their fathers as they made the magnetic passes, could put a roomful of their schoolmates so soundly to sleep that not even a caning by the teacher could arouse them.

The mesmeristic experiments were still continuing in Providence and Newport, and getting more astounding all the time, but Neal was hurrying home to be the first person to put into practice in Maine the manipulatory technique he had learned from that remarkable genius —le docteur le Marquis de Poyen de Sabrieur.

John Greenleaf Whittier had been the first intellectual to make the acquaintance of the versatile Frenchman when as plain Charles Poyen he showed up in Massachusetts. During the fall of 1835 the two young men were often on the road together. Whittier, who had been persuaded by William Lloyd Garrison to run for the legislature on a straight anti-slavery ticket, was working out from Haverhill canvassing sympathetic votes from the downtrodden toilers in the mill towns. Poyen was covering the same territory, giving lessons in French and art to the daughters of the mills' proprietors.

Poyen had not at this time developed his great magnetic powers, but he had lived in Martinique whence his aristocratic family had been forced to flee during the French Revolution. The stories of his island life were music to ears attuned to the thunderings of Garrison. Young Whittier could not get enough of first-hand recitals of the horrors of slavery. Some contemporaries, notably Thomas Nichols, conjectured that the extremely dark foreigner may well have had personal experience on the wrong side of the barracoon himself. Whittier, however, found his atrocity stories more convincing, because more blood-curdling, than the not altogether dissimilar tales of life on their father's plantation in South Carolina as related by those two other fiery protégés of Garrison, Sarah and Angelina Grimke—the first of that hearty line of ladies of the Quaker persuasion who regardless of their meeting-house tenets did so much towards bringing about war.

Whittier encouraged his friend to write down his

thoughts and when "A Philosophical and Historical Essay on Slavery" was completed he recommended it to Garrison and to other forward-looking editors. Mrs. Josepha Hale, then just beginning the career that was to make her America's foremost editress, printed two long excerpts from it in the *Ladies' Magazine*; Dr. William Alcott included a third in his *Annals of Education*. Poyen received no pay for these contributions, but the favorable comment they received was enough to make him wonder if writing could not be made at least as profitable as itinerant teaching.

So on a summer's day in 1836 he hiked to Boston and made the rounds of the publishers' offices, offering to expand his thoughts on slavery into a salable volume. Abolitionist literature was a subject with which every Boston printer was overstocked, but one of them, noticing Poyen's foreign accent and remembering the distinction that Spurzheim's difficulty with English had lent to his lectures, made a counter proposition. Wasn't there, he asked, some other European doctrine that might take on in America as readily as phrenology?

But certainly, Charles Poyen instantly replied. Anton Mesmer's science of animal magnetism had enjoyed much greater fame during Louis XVI's reign than bump feeling in Napoleon's. Mesmer had numbered among his patients the foremost philosophers of Germany, most of the noblemen of Paris, and every beauteous lady at Versailles, Marie Antoinette not excepted.

Whereas the only important person to take up phrenology had been one of Napoleon's lesser mistresses.

To the question as to why America had not heard of the man, Poyen explained that to a scurrilous report on Mesmer's processes, written by a commission of prejudiced, jealous and materialistic French scientists, Minister Benjamin Franklin's signature had unfortunately been appended. But this had not prevented the more enlightened among the aristocracy from forming a Society of Harmony with the purpose of spreading the magnetic influence throughout the continent and over the world. Among the members of this society were the Marquis de Lafayette, the Archbishop of Bordeaux, the Comte de Bourbon, and King Charles X whose first breathless question when he returned with the royal family from exile had been, "Do they still practice magnetism in Paris?"

While pursuing his medical studies at the French Academy Dr. Poyen himself had undergone magnetic treatment for an affliction of the lungs, and as a consequence had become so familiar with the mesmeristic technique that he was prepared to compose an authoritative treatise right on the spot. And *combien* the advance, if you please?

The publisher agreed to print it, but only on one condition—that Dr. Poyen stir up as much excitement over animal magnetism as Dr. Spurzheim had created over phrenology. This was indeed a large order, but thinking it over on his lonely walk home Poyen hit on a possible method of filling it.

IX

Mesmerism Challenges Phrenology as America's Favorite Science

CHARLES POYEN'S MOST SATISFAC-
TORY PATRON WAS A MR. SILAS
WRIGHT, PROPRIETOR OF LOWELL'S
prosperous carpet mill, whose daughters were numerous
and thirsty for culture. During the many hours he had
spent in their home, trying to teach them to draw and
to pronounce French, he had noticed about the premises
a strange female by the name of Gleason.

She had come up from Rhode Island in the first rush
of New England women from the drudgery of the bleak
farms to emancipation in the mills. But being older and
less robust than her fellow seekers after economic freedom, the fourteen-hour day, the poor light and the bad
air in the factory, the skimpiness of the food in the
mill-owned boardinghouses had got her down—but
good. Her eyesight failed, her stomach became strenu-
ously disordered, she developed a consumptive cough
and a nervous affliction that seemed to be a cross between epilepsy and St. Vitus' dance.

She was no more good at carpet-making, but Mr.
Wright, who was a kindly soul, knew that if he discharged her before her two-year apprenticeship was up

she could never get another job. So he had taken her into his own home where for her keep she did whatever odd tasks she was capable of doing. She of course lacked the comeliness of the Parisian ladies upon whom Mesmer and the aristocratic members of the Society of Harmony had wrought their miracles, but she was certainly, Charles Poyen reasoned, no less hysterical.

The next afternoon when he came to give the girls their lessons he suggested to Mrs. Wright that he try to magnetize the Gleason. He did so that night in the presence of the entire gaping family most satisfactorily. He put her in a chair which faced the north, sat down opposite her, and pressed her flat feet with his own. Then he poked his thumbs into the pit of her troubled stomach and stretched his fingers upwards with slow side-to-side movements until they rested near her short ribs. Next he pressed the index finger of his right hand to the summit of her head and drew it down over her face, breast, and lower extremities. Miss Gleason blinked more than customarily.

"Do you sleep?" asked her magnetizer.

"Oui, oui," said Miss Gleason.

The sounds issuing from the contorted face of the unhappy woman brought a moment of intense embarrassment to the members of the household. She had not lapsed into baby-talk, her operator hastily explained. She was now in a state of magnetic somnambulance, unable to see or hear or talk or think with her own organs, but empowered by a wonderful new sense to use his brain and eyes and vocabulary.

"Do you see your disease?" he asked, resuming the tête-à-tête.

"But, yes," said Miss Gleason.

"Then," M. Poyen commanded, "direct the course that is to be followed to preserve your health." And Miss Gleason, lapsing temporarily into English, did so.

When her magnetizer finally awakened her she said she felt lots better but couldn't remember a thing that had happened. Mr. Wright was so impressed by the performance that he agreed to lend her to M. Poyen for a demonstration tour.

During the next several months she was magnetized thousands of times all over New England. She not only repeated the description of her own ailments, but divined obscure, unsuspected afflictions in the members of her audiences, or even in the absent friends and relatives about whom they chanced to think. The correctness of her diagnoses went unquestioned, and the fees from the public demonstrations paid the pair's expenses in the small towns where they put up. Yet during the first months of the tour it seemed highly improbable that mesmerism would seriously challenge phrenology as America's favorite science.

The abolitionists, who had read the Poyen essay and knew of his endorsement by Whittier, came to the demonstrations and spoke well of them. Some even took private lessons and learned to manipulate Miss Gleason's epileptic body and question her entranced mind. But as the strange couple trudged through Massachusetts and Connecticut their reception was in dismal contrast to Spurzheim's triumphant tour. They often struck down-right hostility.

New England wives and mothers outside the abolitionist ranks found something bordering on the scandalous in an unmarried female traveling about openly and unchaperoned with a man who although he looked nice enough might, for all they knew, be up to all kinds of queer goings-on. After all, he was a Frenchman. They refused to go to the public demonstrations, themselves, and made an awful fuss when they caught their men folk taking the manipulatory course in private. The clergy, still haunted by the shade of Cotton Mather, sniffed an odor of brimstone in all this talk about one mind controlling another—though George Wellman, Esquire, a prominent barrister of Taunton, stayed the ministers of that place, who were bent on chasing the mesmerist out of town, by a nice piece of legal logic.

"God meant magnetism to be discovered," Mr. Wellman pointed out to the excited preachers. "If not He would have kept Mesmer from discovering it." Poyen was allowed to show in Taunton, and he used the Wellman phrases effectively whenever he encountered clerical opposition elsewhere.

On this leg of his journey the magnetizer found an eager pupil in a man named Quimby, who in turn instructed the woman who was to found the Christian Science Church. It was, however, the work of two distinguished gentlemen of New York City—Samuel F. B. Morse and William Leete Stone—with whom Poyen was unacquainted, which prepared the way for animal magnetism to become the leading science of the country.

In 1837 Professor Morse at the University of New York demonstrated a device by which he in his laboratory could communicate with an assistant in a room so distant as to be out of ear shot. Though few people could comprehend the scientific principles that controlled his mechanism Professor Morse luckily named it the magnetic telegraph. It lent utter credibility to the feats of animal magnetism. Colonel Stone's literary talents gave them the necessary popular punch.

As a survivor of the old Federalist party, and particularly as the brother-in-law and publishing partner of President Francis Wayland of Brown University, America's foremost educator during three decades, Colonel Stone took his editorial duties with more than common seriousness. His *New York Commercial Advertiser* was dedicated to keeping the new Whig party from degenerating into the rag and bob-tail of the Jacksonian rabble. With colorful invectives he protected the minds of his subscribers from any other radical ideas that might further upset the status quo.

One of the first to feel his wrath was Frances Wright whom he characterized as the Priestess of Beelzebub. When Fanny stepped out of this role by embracing marriage and motherhood, the colonel turned his arsenal of adjectives against the free loveism of John Neal. In the meanwhile, he was conducting a spirited campaign against the strange religious sects that washed in on New York in the wake of Finney's revivals and were particularly offensive to a high vestryman of Trinity Church. Then he turned his attention to the Catholics who were, through their identification with the Irish bloc of Jacksonians, considered fair game by Whig writers.

At the very time Charles Poyen in the Wrights' front parlor was making his first tentative experiment upon Miss Gleason, William Leete Stone, in the interest of journalistic accuracy, had been poking about in the cellar of the Nunnery of the Hotel Dieu in Montreal checking up on the "Awful Disclosures" of Maria Monk.

Miss Monk had showed up at the Bellevue Prison and Hospital just when the New York Magdalene Society, whipped to violent action by the Finney revivals, had partially taken over that institution in its drive to Save All Females Who Have Deviated from the Paths of Virtue. To Arthur Tappan, who on weekdays was New York's richest merchant and on Sundays the Society's most vigilant chaplain, she had told a harrowing tale of her experiences while a novice in the Canadian nunnery. Mr. Tappan had her memoirs published and they became the favorite reading matter of America.

Professor Morse took time off from his telegraphic experiments to head the committee of New York citizens who after questioning the young lady swore to the authenticity of her book. And Colonel Stone went to Montreal to get more details about the lime pit in the cellar of the nunnery where, according to Miss Monk, the nuns tossed their unwanted babies, and the secret passages which connected their beds with a neighboring monastery.

To his political and journalistic chagrin, the colonel found neither pit nor passages. He could unearth nothing to disprove that the Black Nuns of Montreal were pious and respectable. Back in New York he pursued his researches further and discovered that the gravidity of Miss Monk had not been forced upon her by the lechery of a monk but had been come by unresistingly as an ordinary occupational hazard of her business in the Five Points, and that Mr. Tappan had offered her more substantial comfort than kind words as an inducement to stir up indignation against the Catholics. Colonel Stone's book about his findings had for a while a sale almost as great as that of the original fabrications.

When public interest began to lag, and he was seeking a new impostor to expose, he came across an English edition of "The Report of Doctor Benjamin Franklin and the Other Commissioners Charged by the King of France with the Examination of the Animal Magnetism." Through it he learned the true story of Anton Mesmer. Though not unlike the discovery of the Princeton dons concerning Gall and Spurzheim, Colonel Stone's find made more exciting reading.

When in 1779 Anton Mesmer announced that he had discovered "the vehicle of mutual influence between the celestial bodies, the earth, and the bodies of animated beings," and was prepared to cure all disease by this "universally diffused fluid," the medical faculty of the University of Vienna declared that he was no longer fit to practice medicine in Austria. When he disregarded this edict, he was given forty-eight hours in which to get out. There was then as today a handy haven for Austrian quacks. Mesmer crossed into Germany; where his magic met with such sympathetic response from eminent philosophers and scientists that within three years he had enough testimonials to set himself up in Paris.

There one of the first to answer his advertisements concerning his "sovereign instrument for securing the health and lengthening the existence of mankind" was the dissolute seventy-year-old Prince de Soubise, reputed grandson of Louis XIV, who during his more virile years had been the protégé of Madame de Pompadour. His patronage made animal magnetism a fad among the lesser nobility. When Mesmer advertised that for a fee of one hundred louis d'or he would teach the mysteries of his technique to a select group of physicians, among the first hundred doctors to respond was Charles Deslon, member of the Faculty of Medicine and first physician to the brother of Louis XVI who was later King Charles X.

So long as Mesmer had confined his antics to causing

women to become stuck to trees and men to dash their heads against stone walls, and to the gatherings of the Prince de Soubise's crowd and the flibbertigibbets from the lesser mews at Versailles, he attracted no more serious attention than any of the hordes of charlatans that were infesting Paris in 1784. But when Deslon stepped in to become his partner in the serious business of healing, the farce had gone far enough. M. Thoret, first physician to King Louis, pointed out to his patron that the honor of the Faculty of Medicine, if not that of the royal family, was at stake. Louis then appointed the investigating commission composed, in addition to Franklin, of eight of the most distinguished scientists of France, including Guillotin, Bailly, le Roy and Lavoisier.

Franklin was ill at Passy when the examinations began, but when his fellow commissioners saw the writhing, sobbing, erotic frenzies that comprised a magnetic process, they wished him to share the "spectacle." So they took Deslon (who, rather than Mesmer, was their main concern) and an assortment of his patients to Passy. In Franklin's apricot orchard—with his grandsons as pop-eyed witnesses and with some local characters dragged in by his adopted daughter Madame de Brillon to augment the contingent from Paris and add more gaiety to the occasion—the main part of the examination of the animal magnetism took place.

The detailed report of the experiments—infused with the urbane, unstuffy, humorous curiosity of the

most remarkable group of scientists ever gathered together to witness one of the most "wonderful" exhibits
of human absurdity ever recorded—was dutifully laid
before the King; then published for the public. It became a source book for French farces; it caused the
Parisians' admiration of Franklin to rise to adoration;
and it caused the Faculty of Medicine and the Royal
Academy to forbid the practice of mesmerism in France.

Colonel Stone was glad to impart this latest discovery
to his readers. He was less interested in the fact that
the commissioners found animal magnetism non-existent
than in their description of the sumptuous house in Paris
where Mesmer and Deslon practiced their magic.

Why, the colonel informed his readers, it was no
better than a brothel; and got up exactly like one, with
the walls covered by mirrors, a piano-player in the
main salon, and the whole place reeking of aphrodisiacal
perfume. The men and women sat jammed together for
hours around a bucket filled with scrap iron and broken
bottles, holding hands and pressing knees, while twenty
pretty boys maneuvered their bodies in a manner that
Colonel Stone would not defile the pages of his newspaper by describing. He would tell this much, though:
when Mesmer finally appeared among them, decked
out in a peaked cap and a violet robe trimmed with
golden stars and flowers, and waved a glistening miter
over them, they all fell to the floor together and lay
there in a convulsive, moaning, biting, throbbing heap
—until the most far-gone of the women, their stays un-

loosed, were carried off by the young men to the silken-quilted bedrooms called the Apartments of the Crises.

The Protestant clergy, who had been cheated out of their favorite sermon material by Colonel Stone's revelation that the stories about the Black Nunnery just weren't so, found his stories of lechery in atheistic Paris a welcome substitute for lechery in Catholic Montreal. His fellow editors, whose practice it was to fill up their own papers by elaborating on items that had appeared in their rivals', took advantage of the *Commercial Advertiser's* low-down on Mesmer. They outdid one another in calling the long-dead Austrian names like fraud, fake, humbug and monster. They were still adding details of their own imagining to his notorious séance room when to their surprise this Card signed by its editor appeared in large type on the front page of the *Commercial Advertiser*:

"We have had our time laughing at Animal Magnetism. We shall laugh no more. With our own eyes we have witnessed results that are not only marvelous, but absolutely astounding. We venture to state that nothing hitherto published on the subject is so wonderful by far."

X

The Conversion of Colonel Stone

THE WHOLE OF GOTHAM AND WHIG-
DOM WAS BREATHLESS TO DISCOVER
WHAT HAD MADE COLONEL STONE
change fronts. The causes were many and complicated,
but the first of them was that M. Poyen had taken Miss
Gleason as far south as Rhode Island and met with an
unexpectedly gracious reception.

Newport in the summer of 1837, striving to become
as exclusive as Saratoga, the White Sulphur and Rock-
away, was the last community that could have been
expected to welcome the strange pair. But George
Henry Calvert had been in Paris when magnetism came
out of hiding. Lafayette had smarted when Louis XVI,
chiding him on his credulity, had asked, "What will
Washington think of your embracing magnetism?" But
Louis was gone then as well as most of the famous
heads of the commission, fallen beneath the invention
of a colleague; and the magnetic fluid was flowing un-
obstructed. Lafayette welcomed young Calvert into the
international set that comprised the Society of Harmony. Its titled members treated him like a spiritual
brother.

He now extended the same courtesies to the dazed
M. Poyen and the quaking Miss Gleason; and got busy
writing a treatise on mesmerism which he knew his
aspiring New England friends would treat kindlier
than the Baltimoreans had his exposition of phrenology.
The ladies of Newport were, of course, delighted to
embrace the science that had brought romantic Marie
Antoinette such pleasure.

It was while listening to Mr. Calvert's reminiscences
of his Parisian days that Charles Poyen recollected his
own title of Marquis de Sabrieur. This, added to the
doctorate he had assumed in his agreement with the
Boston printer, made him an imposing figure. Fortified
socially and academically he proceeded to Providence,
and received an ovation not unlike that tendered Spurzheim in New Haven and Boston. All seventeen physicians of the town and the faculty of Brown signed up
for the courses in manipulations.

President Wayland was so busy attending the séances
that he did not have time to read his brother-in-law's
editorials. Thus it came about that Francis Wayland was
writing to his academic colleagues to tell them that
magnetism was the most wonderful science extant at
the same time William Leete Stone was dubbing it the
biggest humbuggery in Christendom. This was indeed
a situation and no one realized it more than President
Wayland. As soon as the public began to compare his
version of mesmerism with the Colonel's either the
Commercial Advertiser or Brown University would be-

come the target of derision; and Francis Wayland had big stakes in both enterprises.

In his extremity he sought the guidance of an old friend and fellow alumnus of Union College, the Right Reverend Thomas Brownell, who was fortunately visiting in Providence at the time. Bishop Brownell had been exalted to the episcopate of Connecticut from Trinity Church and knew how to deal with his former parishioner. He placed his august personage before his escritoire and wrote Colonel Stone a stiff note. If he would only come up to Rhode Island and see with his own eyes the wonders of magnetism he would, the Bishop guaranteed, feel less "sarcastical" about the subject.

Bulled into action, Colonel Stone caught the next boat up the Sound, but by the time he arrived later developments in the progress of magnetism had occurred. Poyen had already left Providence in a huff because the local physicians, claiming to have developed mesmeristic powers far stronger than his own, had stopped taking his manipulatory courses. These gentlemen had discovered among their own patients magnetic subjects whose diagnostic abilities far outdistanced Miss Gleason's. There was some rivalry about which of the Providence doctors should demonstrate before Colonel Stone. The Episcopalians thought the honor should go to Dr. Pardon Brownell, for he was the Bishop's brother, but the Brownells themselves decided in favor of Dr.

George Capron, a Baptist, because he possessed in the person of Miss Loraina Brackett the perfect subject.

While seated at her loom some time since Miss Brackett suffered the misfortune of having an iron weight of several pounds fall from a considerable elevation to the crown of her head. The injury was so severe as to deprive her almost of her life and entirely of her reason for several months, during which time she was subject to the most serious derangements of her nervous system and lost both her sight and her voice. Arrangements had been made to send her to Dr. Howe's Blind School when Dr. Capron's passes restored some of her senses. She recovered her voice and the ability to tell light from darkness, and developed unexpectedly wondrous powers of clairvoyance.

She could read sealed letters from a distance through three thicknesses of paper and describe the contents of pictures which were balanced, of all places, on the top of her head. She originated the idea of having those with whom she was *en rapport* take her on ideal or imaginary journeys to distant places she had never visited. At the very time Colonel Stone was arriving in Providence, for example, one of her callers was conducting her to Saratoga Springs. She admired the hotels of the resort and the costumes of the resorters, but when she stopped at the Congress fountain she contorted her bashed features and spat out the imaginary water.

Another young gentleman had been so incautious as

to take her to Cuba by steamboat. That trip, however, was too rough for her delicate constitution and the results of her seasickness were realized in the young gentleman's lap.

Dr. Capron now sat beside her and began his magnetic maneuvers. Colonel Stone, remembering what he himself had written about the goings-on in Paris, watched him closely and was relieved to note that he manipulated her in a manner that was neither disagreeable nor objectionable but on the contrary positively *refined*. In a few minutes the young lady was in a deep slumber, sensible to the presence of no one save Dr. Capron. After putting her through her picture-identifying and letter-reading paces, he gave her a particular introduction to the visitor from New York, and endowed him with the power of enjoying her exclusive company.

For a few minutes the two who were now in perfect rapprochement conversed upon ordinary subjects, and Colonel Stone was immediately impressed by the sprightliness of Miss Brackett's intelligence and the elegance of English in which her remarks were couched. Knowing that she had never been to New York he asked her if she would accompany him there and describe Castle Garden, Trinity Church, the Astor House and his own home on Church Street.

She agreed prettily, but remembering her mal-de-mer added, "I would like to go through the air."

Colonel Stone assured her that he would as gladly accompany her that way as any other.

"But you must not let me fall," said she.

"Oh, no," said he, with quick wit but not entire veracity, "I am used to that way of traveling and will bear you up in perfect safety."

She then grasped his hands more firmly and pressed upon them tremulously as if buoying herself up. Colonel Stone then very slowly raised his hands ten or twelve inches, favoring the idea that she was ascending.

"You must keep me up," she said with a slight convulsive or rather shuddering gasp, as though apprehensive of a fall.

"Certainly," her flying partner replied. "You need have no fear. I am used to these excursions." And away in imagination they sailed:

"Oh," Miss Brackett cried happily, "how I like to travel this way—so easy and we go so quick."

"Yes," her companion answered, "and here we are in New York. Come, we will descend at the north end of the Battery."

He then proposed that they step into Castle Garden. She acquiesced and to his surprised delight she also appeared to act cautiously as if experiencing the sensations of stepping upon a bridge. He spoke up quickly, assuring her that the bridge was quite safe and that since he held a season ticket they could go straight into the Garden. But still the modest young lady demurred and called his attention to a man at the gate who she felt sure would not let them through.

"He is a constable, a police officer," Colonel Stone

explained. "But he knows me well, and will open the gate for us."

At this a smile played over Miss Brackett's features. "Why," she cried out in pleasure, "what a queer hat he has got on."

How did she mean "queer"? Colonel Stone wanted to know. What did the hat look like?

"Why," she answered, a little miffed at his tone, "it's a large round hat with a low crown, like a Quaker's."

This reply nettled Colonel Stone considerably, for anyone, even if she had never been to New York and even if she had had a heavy weight fall on the crown of her head, should know that the New York constabulary wore no such outlandish headgear as she described. "What sort of a coat has he on?" he asked. "Or is it a jacket?"

"It is a round jacket," she replied immediately. And Colonel Stone had the explanation of her mistake. He had spoken too quickly and hurried her too much. The bridge upon which he had assisted her was not that which led to the Garden proper but to the Castle Garden Boat Club. She had been describing the costume of one of the members who, even at this hour of the morning, was no doubt somewhere about the place.

Miss Brackett's next remark after he got her to her destination also pleased her escort. "It does not seem much like a garden," she said.

"Very true," he agreed. "It was an old fort which has been fitted up as a place of amusement. They get up

grand displays of fireworks at night on festival occasions. At other times people come here to get fresh air,
drink lemonade and punch, and smoke segars."

But Miss Brackett said she was afraid of fireworks
and disapproved of smoking, and stated calvinistically,
"I choose not to go in."

"As you say," Colonel Stone replied, disappointed
but still gallant. "We will turn about and walk up
town. Now we are on the Battery. How do you like the
trees?"

Miss Brackett said she admired them very much.
She expressed the same sentiment in regard to Bowling
Green Park, Mechanics Hall and Mr. Ray's house,
which Colonel Stone called to her attention as they
went strolling by. Yet he was again perplexed. Although the Ray home was on the right of anyone walking *up* Broadway, she stared steadily to the left as she
admired it. Her guide remonstrated with her about
this, and she proved herself to possess as quick a wit as
she had been credited with.

"To be sure it's on the right," she said. "But you do
hurry me so. Just now you hurried me so that I was
turned round and walking back down the street." And
she added archly, "When a gentleman walks with me
I don't like for him to be impatient."

Colonel Stone and the other guests in the drawing-
room were charmed at that cute little dig. President
Wayland laughed the loudest of any of them and said

it was a fact, often remarked in the family, that his brother-in-law was a terrifically impatient walker.

When the hilarity had died down the young lady, with set lips, continued to stare fixedly over her left shoulder, but refused to describe what she saw. Colonel Stone was at a loss as to how to proceed and conferred with the rest of the group. Miss Brackett's admiring friends had a ready explanation: her delicacy. One so modest as she would be sure to glimpse in the regions of Lower Broadway sights which would shock her, and it was unthinkable that she would mention them to a person of the opposite sex.

Colonel Stone was delighted with the explanation and to rectify her opinion of the city led her into Trinity Church. She said the pews certainly were in a terrible condition. As soon as he got back to New York the colonel verified this observation and brought it sharply to the attention of the vestry.

Out on Broadway again Miss Brackett delighted her companion by exclaiming, "I never saw people crowd so. Why, they run over a body without the least care." And she began to shrink and to edge sidewise as though jostled by a throng. From this he knew that they must be approaching the Astor House. When this was pointed out to her she stopped, gazed up and around as if taking a deliberate survey of the building, and said, "Large!"

When asked how many stories there were she began to point and apparently to count. Colonel Stone thought she reached "Five" which was indeed the correct answer, but when he urged her to speak out more loudly she refused to do so. She also refused to go inside the building, saying she did not think it proper to patronize a hotel owned by an old man who cheated the Indians by adding his fist to the weight of their furs, and besides, there were so many men there. Though her escort was finding her scruples a little trying he was highly pleased with this observation, because the Astor House *was* crowded at this time of day; indeed it was crowded at any time.

By now the sightseers had got as far as Park Place and Colonel Stone proposed that they turn into Church Street and stop by his house as he had some daguerreotypes in his study that he wanted to show her. Miss Brackett said she admired the trees in his big yard very much and that his house was very large, but that it was shut up, so how could they go in?

This disconcerted the colonel, for his house was a compact three-story affair, flush with the street in front and with only a flag-stone court, innocent of trees, in the back. Although he was too much of a gentleman to say so, he must have suspected that Miss Brackett wasn't quite so innocent as she seemed, but had heard that old daguerreotype gag before and was having him on.

Then he realized that in spite of her remonstrance he had hurried her again, rushed her clear to the bottom of Church Street and to the Green of Columbia College. The large house she had seen, and taken for his, was

[111]

the college building with its many wings, now closed for summer vacation. So describing his own modest dwelling he piloted her back up the street and asked her to enter and tell him what the servants were doing now that they were alone in the house without supervision.

After a few minutes Miss Brackett emerged from the basement and reported that they were doing nothing, but added that they frightened her because they were black. This was odd, for all three of the Stones' maids were pink-faced girls newly come from Ireland. Once more the experiment seemed to have hit an impasse. But once more Colonel Stone recollected his habit of impatience, and decided it was again at fault. He must have rushed his companion back up Church Street as rapidly as he had hurried her down it in the first place. While he was collecting his wits she had already reached the corner of Park Place again and got into the residence of Mr. Douglass who was the only householder in the block who employed Negro servants.

Catching up with her at last, Colonel Stone guided her resolutely back to No. 36, where she still insisted that his maids, though of light complexion, were definitely idle. This was a slight error, for it was Monday and all three were elbows deep in suds, but Colonel Stone was so relieved that Miss Brackett had stopped barging into strange houses that he did not bother to correct her. Instead, he showed her through his home and asked her to describe the pictures in the various rooms. This she refused flatly to do saying, "Why, that is silly. You know what they are as well as I do."

Colonel Stone was stymied for fair. He returned Miss Brackett's hands, and her magnetized mind, to Dr. Capron who burst in upon her consciousness with a hearty, "Why, Miss Brackett, whatever are you doing in New York?"

And Miss Brackett, not at all disconcerted to be found in what less modest ladies might consider a compromising position, said she was having a lovely time visiting with Colonel Stone who had just been showing her some pictures. Then under Dr. Capron's skillful questioning she described these pictures with uncanny accuracy, saying that the one over the sideboard in the dining-room seemed to portray fruit—or vegetables, game or fish; and the one which hung above the Bible-table in the parlor gave her a religious feeling.

This crucial test convinced William Leete Stone that animal magnetism was indeed a science and that the Church of England had been misled by the skeptical French into dubbing it a fraud. To guard against his backsliding when he got among his scoffing friends in New York again, Bishop Brownell made him sit right down in President Wayland's office and write up the experiment exactly as it had occurred. To make sure that the report would reach the scientific and academic audience for which it was intended, Colonel Stone titled his seventy-five-page printed monograph "A Letter to

Dr. A. A. Bingham," the Columbia professor who had been Spurzheim's original sponsor.

A few days after receiving the "Letter" from his next-door neighbor, Dr. Bingham replied, also in form suitable for publication, that having made the necessary experiments himself, he was as convinced as Colonel Stone, President Wayland, Bishop Brownell, Bishop Potter, and President Nott of Union College, that Mesmer's discoveries were as authentic as Gall's and Spurzheim's. Governor Benjamin Parke and the lawmakers in Harrisburg, proud of their prestige as the first public officials to be felt by the Fowlers, founded a Committee on Magnetism to start the fluid flowing through Pennsylvania. The phrenologists of Boston, however, jealous of their fame as the owners of Spurzheim's cadaver, withheld their endorsement until the new science could be demonstrated to them by a non-American.

Dr. Robert Collyer of Edinburgh, with an endorsement from Charles Dickens who was also speaking in Boston at the time, satisfied that requirement; and the same physicians, professors and ministers who had immortalized Spurzheim met at the Masonic Temple to watch him perform. As was his custom, Dr. Collyer produced his own Scots boy and started to go to work on him. But at the insistence of Dr. Winslow Lewis and Dr. Francis Dana, on guard against collusion, he substituted Frederick, a protégé of Dr. Calvin Stowe, who suffered from both epilepsy and St. Vitus' dance.

Dr. Collyer put Frederick in touch with Mr. Parke, a medical student at Harvard, who had the correctly sympathetic vibrations. Mr. Parke thought of the Charlestown jail; and Frederick said, "It's cold." Mr. Parke's mind then fastened upon the round tub which is placed in every cell for necessary purposes. Frederick looked beseechingly for the Reverend Mr. Stowe, ducked his shaking head and said, "It's nasty. I don't want to tell."

The faculty of mathematics at Harvard calculated the probability of his giving that particular response, when Mr. Parke thought of that particular object, down almost to the very same goose egg that the faculty of mathematics at Duke University is arriving at today to re-prove animal magnetism under the newer name of extra-sensory perception.

XI

Cora Mowatt—
19th Century Glamour Girl

WHEN THE MOST DISTINGUISHED
MEMBERS OF THE MASSACHU-
SETTS BAR HANDED DOWN THE
opinion that the evidence taken at the Masonic Temple
was more strictly from Blackstone than that picked up
in Poor Richard's backyard in Passy, Mesmer was given
in the hierarchy of the gods of New England intellectuals a place on the right hand of Spurzheim as exalted
as that occupied by Carlyle, Swedenborg, Goethe and
Priessnitz. And magnetism was quickly adapted to typically American uses.

Lawyers used it for abstracting testimony from balky
witnesses. Longfellow's dear friend, Charles Bonneville, resigned his professorship at Harvard to teach
the mesmeristic technique to the Mormons. Joseph
Smith had found phrenology very helpful in picking his
Saints, and Professor Bonneville knew magnetism
would be as serviceable in keeping plural wives in hand.

John Pierpont made the magnetic maneuvers inval-
uable to ministers. When paying a pastoral call he
would take a little tyke of four or five upon his knee—

as his great grandson and namesake less expertly dandled a midget—and, while apparently fondling the lad, put him into a deep trance. Then the little one, lisping words he surely could not have understood, would diagnose his own or his sister's stomachache or the spiritual troubles of his parents.

It was Mrs. Cora Ogden Mowatt who gave to mesmerism the artistic feminine appeal that the Fowlers' demonstrations in Troy had given phrenology. She was a very different type of magnetic subject from Miss Brackett and Miss Gleason, and would no more have dreamed of working in a cotton factory than of using the products of such a place. She was strictly silks and satins—the outstanding glamour girl of the middle nineteenth century. Her family trees contained just the right mixture of Episcopal ministers and Declaration of Independence signers and her father was so well off financially that a trial for treason did not impair his social standing.

At fourteen Anna Cora Ogden was thrilled to envy when from a box at the Park Theater she saw Fanny Kemble's farewell performance in the "Hunchback." She was thrilled too when handsome James Mowatt, her composition teacher, told her tenderly that his dearest wish was to be her instructor throughout eternity. This young reader of law had turned his attentions to thirteen-year-old Cora when he discovered that like himself she had literary ambitions and a flair for amateur theatricals; and by the time he proposed he had helped her write half a novel. To complete the volume on her honeymoon with James, Cora was willing to forego the elaborate début her father had planned for her; but Papa was not.

Samuel Ogden, though he had risked his good name and his neck by plotting to pilfer all the gold in Spanish America, could not fly in the face of fashion to the extent of not having his handsomest daughter come out. Since there was no law in New York State to keep a woman of fourteen from marrying whom she wished, he notified Bishop Onderdonk that he would withdraw the handsome donation he had promised toward building that new church up at Broadway and Tenth Street unless the good bishop forbade every clergyman in the parish to marry the self-willed chit. So Cora and James had to sneak off in the night and be wedded by a Free Churcher down below Bleeker Street.

For six years after this, with a reluctant parental blessing, they lived like any other wealthy young couple in fashionable Flatbush. Then, especially after James' law practice failed to materialize, they became restless for fame. Finally one night in 1841 after attending a reading by the elder Vanderhoof they came to a decision. Maybe it would not be quite proper for an American matron as well born as Cora to go directly on the stage of the Park, as the manager of that theater had so long been urging her to do, but surely public readings in the dignified Vanderhoof manner would not be infra dig. Only, Cora put in, she was certainly going to open in Boston which, although she had never seen it, was by the common consent of its inhabitants the American Athens.

Her reading of the "Lay of the Last Minstrel" at the Tremont Temple was the expected success. After the performance her retiring-room was crowded. Professor Longfellow asked her girlhood friend Julia Ward, now married to Dr. Samuel Howe of the Blind School, to introduce him, and sent Cora a note complimenting the charm of her scanning.

The show in Providence the next week was even better. At the climax of her reading of "The Missing Ship," a dramatization of the sinking of the *S.S. President* which Epes Sargeant, America's foremost dramatist, had written especially for her, three ladies screamed hysterically, fainted dead away, and had to be carried from the hall. Her pleasure in her triumph was not dimmed by learning that all three were patients of Dr. Capron and therefore particularly allergic to boat-rides.

After this build-up, the mental suffering caused by the unexpected reception she got in her home town was acute. The morning after her début at the Stuyvesant Institute when she went for her customary walk on Broadway she was pointedly snubbed, not just by childhood friends but by her own kin. The New York papers were not satisfied with condemning her enunciation and delivery, but repeated the calumnious tales told by her erstwhile friends—that Cora Ogden had been the biggest show-off at the Leroy Place Seminary and had married Mr. Mowatt just because he promised to get her on the stage. *The Ladies' Companion,* to which she had contributed casually since her marriage, remarked acidly that if she *must* give public readings she could at least read entirely before audiences of her own sex.

Not even the dedicatory poem of dear Mrs. Osgood —which began:

> Ne'er heed them, Cora dear,
> The carping few, who say
> Thou leavest woman's holiest sphere
> For light and vain display

—could mitigate the soul sickness that the unkindness of New York brought upon her. After four performances she collapsed. The hastily summoned physician pronounced her recovery improbable unless she gave up the readings.

Cora agreed with him; it was a way to save her face if not her life. Back at the Astor House, under the care of the Ogden family doctor, she remembered the stories told her in Providence about Dr. Capron's lady patients. Perhaps, she whispered, magnetic treatment might help a little. Her physician listened to her pretty pleas, and found that she was so sensitive to the influence that she could be put to sleep in less than one-fourth of a minute.

Having swayed hundreds by her recitations, she had no idea, even to save her life, of surrendering her will to her magnetizer, as if she were an humble mill drudge. So she made a bargain with him. He would come around to the Astor House at two o'clock each day, renew whatever passes were necessary to keep her in the magnetic state for another twenty-four hours, and let her name the time of awakening. To make sure that she would always be "the dictator" in the mesmeristic alliance, she insisted that the doctor stay to dinner which at the Astor was served in the Ladies' Ordinary at three o'clock.

Though in her somnambulant state her eyelids hung loose and the balls of her eyes were so rolled as to render them useless as a medium of vision, she was so much the master of the magnetic influence that she described every dish the doctor selected from the Card, even to fresh strawberries which were served, and quite unexpectedly, the first time of the year that day. But she refused to eat anything herself, saying, "The simpleton (the term her magnetic mind used for her material body) isn't hungry." As the physician, departing for his afternoon calls, gave a few pills to her husband, she cautioned him, "No drugs. Perhaps magnetism will bring her through. She will have her crisis at eight o'clock. She will awaken before then, but will fall asleep again before the crisis."

Just as her magnetic mind had predicted, the simpleton awoke soon after the doctor left, feeling very chipper indeed, and with no knowledge of the ominous conversation. Her husband and the other dinner guests were afraid to inform her of the impending crisis, lest

realization of it should aggravate her condition. As
eight o'clock approached she insisted, quite innocently,
on going down to the parlor. There at the destined
hour, surrounded not only by her friends but strangers
from out of town, an expression of intense pain overcame her features, and she fell back in a violence of
convulsive writhings fearful to witness. Her forehead
throbbed, her skin became of fever heat, horrible spasms
played through her limbs, and her face grew first pale
and then curiously luminous. It was an hour before she
relaxed. Then a smile of inexpressible sweetness broke
over her shining countenance as she whispered to herself, "You have brought her through."

Of course after the crisis was past there was no urgent
necessity for keeping Mrs. Mowatt magnetized any
longer. Yet her husband and family agreed that the
treatments had best be kept up, since under their influence she was less susceptible to colds, and also more
manageable and reliable. Indeed, while mesmerized her
whole demeanor changed. Her voice became soft and
infantine and all her mannerisms those of a child.

She was especially humane toward the more despised
of God's creatures, manifesting toward spiders and all
other insects, from which in her waking state she would
shrink affrighted, a strange and fearless tenderness. The
guests at the Astor House could hope for no braver
sight—though the management did not concur—than
beautiful Mrs. Mowatt, with her curls crisp and her
eyelids drooping, groping along the corridors for what-

ever despised brutes the hostelry harbored. And when perchance her bejeweled hand rested upon a wounded spider, a one-winged fly or an inadequately squashed Croton bug—that's when the management's jitters approached the screaming stage—she would pick it up with a tenderness, which in anyone else might have been deemed simple-mindedness, and remove it to her room.

The management, however, found compensation in her condition—it saved them precious quantities of illuminating gas. Since she did not need her natural eyes to find her way around in the daytime, neither did she at night. Her husband thought it rather homey to sit in the dark, unable to see their hands before them, and hear her tidying up the suite without bumping into more than an occasional piece of furniture. The hem-stitching that she did in the pitch blackness was much admired, her chirography far superior to her usual careless scrawl, and she could read with her eyes closed more intelligibly than when they were open. At first, though, her husband was a little testy about the books she chose to read aloud to him hours after every other young couple in New York had their lamps lit.

Being by both birth and education of a skeptical turn of mind he preferred the current works of his fellow-men-about-town, Epes Sargeant, Laughton Osborn and Nathaniel P. Willis. But she would read nothing but Swedenborg. After a while, through endless listenings, he became interested enough in immortal planes and celestial spheres to inform Cora that he was willing to join the New Church. To his vast surprise—he seemed a little slow in catching on—Cora, who happened at the moment to be the simpleton, became jocose and said she knew nothing about Swedenborg and, even if she did, she thought he was an old bore.

When her physician was consulted about the discrepancy between Cora's magnetized and waking attitudes toward Heaven and Hell, he said there was nothing to be done about that particular problem but to wait until she was strong enough to wrestle with such mighty thoughts, when Mr. Mowatt could convert her as patiently as she had him. In general, though, the physician added, he did believe that Mrs. Mowatt was overdoing the magnetism a little, staying entranced longer than was really good for her. This was soon borne out when she insisted on remaining out of this world for two solid weeks.

When she finally agreed to be awakened the snow which had blanketed New York when she went to sleep was all gone, and the rose bush in her room, which had been budless when she had last seen it, was now in full bloom. Her agitation at these unexpected sights was so great that her life was again feared for, and the physician had to make quick and vigorous passes to get her quiet again. He then gave her an ordination to carry over into her waking state so much recollection of her fortnight's experience as would prepare her fully for the changes around her. He also suggested to Mr. Mowatt that from this time on he place his hand on his wife's forehead whenever she began to wake up and think of everything that had happened while she was asleep. The scheme worked beautifully. Mrs. Mowatt's mind responded to her husband's reminiscent fingers as perfectly and accurately as the keys of a piano; she knew everything she had done or said while in her stupor.

It was indeed fortunate that she did, for during the three years in which the greater part of her life was somnambulant, she was the busiest lady in all New York. She wrote regularly for *Godey's, Graham's, The Democratic Review* and *The Ladies' Companion.* With *The Fortune Hunter,* a satirical novel about high society in which she got back at those false friends who had snubbed her almost to her death, she won the $100 prize offered by Park Benjamin and Rufus Griswold of the *New World,* the highest literary award of 1842.

The books of advice to ladies which she compiled in her spare time turned out to be so profitable that her husband established a printing firm for their exclusive publication. Since most of them were produced during the period when she was flitting back and forth from the ethereal state, without any clear idea of just where she was, she never knew what all of them were about. A few titles of which she was conscious were:

> *Housekeeping Made Easy*
> *Book of the Toilette*
> *Cookery for the Sick*
> *The Book of Embroidery*

The Mad Forties

Knitting, Netting and Crochet
Etiquette for Ladies
Ballroom Etiquette
The Etiquette of Matrimony

On top of all this, with the ever-ready assistance of Epes Sargeant, she wrote and produced the comedy *Fashion* which poked fun at the outlanders who tried to crash New York society. Every critic in the city except Edgar Allan Poe, who said it bore the same relation to *Love for Love* as the shell of a locust to the living beast, pronounced it better than Congreve. Finally and inevitably she allowed the manager of the Park Theater to persuade her to appear upon the stage. Whereupon she was instantly proclaimed the American Fanny Kemble.

Thus the Brenda Frazier of her day had become a Pearl Buck, an Emily Post, a Clare Boothe, and finally, a Katharine Cornell, all rolled into one package—a package neat enough to fill a Hollywood sweater.

Mrs. Mowatt was too inclusive in her boast that every female in America with a yearning for etiquette, the stage or the novel, detested her for her achievements in these fields. Mary Gove was a notable exception.

She and John Neal were struck by one phase of Mrs. Mowatt's magnetic experience that had been lost on the sensation-loving public: the preliminary fact that she had refused to turn over her mind to her magnetizer. This proved to them incontestably that a woman, even

when bereft of her normal faculties, was no more weak-
minded than man. The practical application of this fact
to Mrs. Gove's own determination to become a healer
was obvious.

Though her sex barred her from the allopathic and
conservative medical colleges, it would not keep her
from learning the manipulatory technique of mesmerism. Then she would no longer be the mere recipient of
world-saving visions. She could impress her ideals on
less fortunate minds for their own good. She was about
to renounce the static science of phrenology for the
dynamics of magnetism when John Pierpont told her
that would be unnecessary. Dr. Joseph Rodes Buchanan
of Transylvania University had already combined the
best features of the two techniques in a perfectly marvelous manner.

XII

Testing Man's Impressibility

THE COLLEGES SURGING UP TO THE WEST WERE AN EMBARRASSMENT TO THE GRADUATES OF THE universities of New England. Not only were Center, Cincinnati, George Washington and the rest, larger, because aided by public funds, than Yale and Harvard, but Transylvania's very existence mitigated the honor that had come to those institutions because of their intimate contact with Spurzheim.

In 1821 Charles Taylor Caldwell, founder of Transylvania's medical department, had gone to Europe with $10,000 allocated by the State of Kentucky to acquire for that projected university the first library of the West. While there he had picked up besides the books an acquaintance with the fundamentals of phrenology. Upon his return he had functioned in Lexington, Louisville, and the other western towns as the "American Spurzheim."

For ten years this fact had made no impression one way or another upon the scholars in the East, but after the real Spurzheim's death, the priority to the title had become a real botherment to all the Yales and Harvards who wanted to assume it for themselves. Sectional jealousy, however, had not prevented John Pierpont from acclaiming the accomplishments of Professor Buchanan when, as scientific heir to Caldwell, the Transylvania phrenologist came to Boston to demonstrate his discovery of the organ of Magnetic Impressibility.

It was not really a new organ, but a hitherto unexplored region of that section of the cranium which was designated on most charts as Physical Sensibility. Though this bump, which controlled the external senses, was prominently situated in the temple just over the cheek, most phrenologists had neglected it in favor of the more dignified rear organs where the Knowing Faculties and the Sentiments Proper to Man were located. They usually described it as that part of the brain which made men as well as animals sensitive to touch, taste, smell, hearing and sight—and let it go at that.

Professor Buchanan, primarily a medical man, became particularly interested in the Organ of Physical Sensibility because, being relatively unprotected, it was "fortunately often injured"—especially in his native West, where fist-fights, bitings and buttings, rather than the effete pistols of the East, were the accepted means of settling personal grievances. Pursuing his researches on patients who had been knocked cold by heavy blows on the temple and cheek bone, Dr. Buchanan confirmed the hypothesis that it was through the *lower* section of the Organ of Sensibility that a man felt heat, cold, dryness, light, sound, etc. But the higher portion, which connected with Somnolence, Modesty and Ideality, had, he felt sure, a different and much less mundane function. It responded only to the human Nervaura which were the scientific elements underlying the magnetic influence. Thus the Organ of Nervauric Impressibility gave a physiological basis to magnetism and made it a branch of the only true science of the mind—phrenology.

Not all persons possessed the Organ of Nervauric Impressibility to the same degree, Dr. Buchanan pointed out, and estimated that the population of the South was some three or four times as impressible as that of the North. Since he had boasted of fancy Virginia forebears, he felt constrained to declare that Nervauric Sensibility in no way implied mental weakness, but was highly congenial to intellectuality, and was occasionally found in the strongest and most cultivated minds.

Dr. Buchanan not only demonstrated Nervauric Sensibility in his own patients but wrote a long and learned treatise explaining how anyone could test his friends for its possession. The process was complicated and slightly terrifying.

If you suspect an acquaintance of being susceptible, you ask him to stand without support in the middle of a large room. You then reach up and place your finger gently on the spot just above and slightly behind the brow where Nervauric Sensibility blends with Somnolence. If your friend winks, droops his lids, closes his eyes, and, conditions being favorable, emits a mild snore, you are ready for the real test. Very quietly you withdraw your hands, and holding them before you, slowly back away from him. If his head follows your fingers until his rigid body lies prostrate on the floor, you can be certain that his Organ of Magnetic Impressibility has become violently aroused and is lending its excitement to the whole brain. In this condition the subject becomes a kind of psychic seismograph, sensitive to the magnetic influences—or, in the unnecessarily cumbersome language of the gestalt psychologists, of the dynamical interaction of the psychic stresses and strains—emanating from all animate and inanimate objects.

If, for instance, a subject thus impressibly aroused put his hand on the chest of a man of vigorous constitution he immediately became stronger and more energetic. If, instead, his palm rested for as long as twenty minutes against the stomach of a diseased person he became so ill that strong dispensive passes were necessary to restore him to normal health. The danger of some hitch in the proceedings leaving the subject permanently and incurably diseased was so great that Dr. Buchanan would never demonstrate this particular experiment upon "any but those embarrassed by a constitutional skepticism which hinders their believing anything not impressed on their own sensibilities."

A non-skeptical subject, however, could sicken himself almost to death just by touching his operator—

provided, of course, his finger landed on the exact spot in the cranium that covered the phrenological Organ of Disease. If from there his thumb strayed to Mirth he would if that organ happened to be large let out a loud guffaw; should it be small he would giggle, and if exceptionally tiny, merely simper. Then touching one after the other all the bumps of the higher mental and moral faculties he would act out each thought and impulse of his vis-à-vis. Thus a nervauric subject could within a few minutes make a complete and infallible analysis of the mind, character, and probable vocational fitness, of a perfect stranger.

Dr. Buchanan called this particular phase of his larger science of nervaurism "psychometry." The aptitude tests, through which the vocational psychologists practice psychometry today, seem merely to complicate and render more mysterious his candid and straightforward technique.

Like consulting psychologists and vocational guides, Dr. Buchanan also laid great stress on chirography; but again his method was simpler and more direct. An impressible subject had merely to place his hand upon a written word to receive the nervauric impulses that the writer had imparted to it. Since even death did not interfere with this nervauric contact, Dr. Buchanan was sure that as soon as the sensitive fingers of impressible subjects replaced the bespectacled eyes and dry brains of scholars, as the accepted tools of research, "facts of history and biography never before attainable, or even dreamed of, will soon be discovered."

As for the contributions of impressibility to medical research, they were almost limitless. Obviously a nervauric subject could diagnose diseases much more accurately than ordinary medical men, or even Miss Gleason. Their pharmaceutical powers were even more practical. Let one of them hold a vial of liquid in his hand, and without seeing, tasting or smelling it, his body would show all its effects much more quickly than if he had swallowed it—even though it be a newly invented concoction that had never before come in contact with a human lip. It was necessary, of course, when making such tests, for the operator to be especially alert and ready for the dispensive passes in case the vial prove to contain poison.

Although Professor Buchanan described all these experiments so clearly that the rankest amateur could perform them, he warned all except the most practiced operator against undertaking them. The danger lay in the circumstance that the novice operator might be as impressible as his subject. Thus as each got nervauric impulses from the other's chest, stomach and head, their characters and personalities would become so entangled and intermingled that they might never be able to unscramble their separate selves again.

Since at the time he disclosed his data Dr. Buchanan was the only experienced nervauric operator in the world, it was necessary for him to demonstrate his method personally and publicly. This he did with pleas-ant success before scientific groups in Louisville, Cincinnati and the cultural centers of the West. He then came to Boston to show off to John Pierpont who sent him with his apostolic blessing to New York.

The scientific commission who waited upon him there was headed by Orson and Lorenzo Fowler, representing the College of Phrenologists, the Reverend LaRoy Sunderland for the Society of Magnetizers, and William Cullen Bryant for the Homeopathic College. Bryant, especially impressed by his contributions to materia medica, joined the Fowlers in proclaiming Dr. Buchanan as warmly as John Pierpont had. But Dr. Sunderland in the interest of the magnetizers entered a demurrer.

There seemed never to have been a period in LaRoy Sunderland's life when he was not a central figure in some violent clash of ideas. Back in the early 1830's such was his eloquence that the Methodists were grooming him as their most likely contender for the title, then held by the Presbyterians' Charles G. Finney, of the country's most persuasive evangelist. Preacher Sunderland belabored Satan mightily, but he delivered harder oratorical punches against the slave-holders at the South. He even dared attack those members of his own denomination in the North, among them some of the most prominent bishops, who expressed the opinion that there might be means short of war for settling the abolition question. The bishops, after pleading with him in the name of denominational unity to moderate his views, renounced and unfrocked him.

Deprived of a pulpit, LaRoy Sunderland moved to New York, perfected himself in modern science and developed magnetic powers even more forceful than his oratorical strength. He was prospering at his new profession when there appeared a novel called *Confessions of a Magnetizer*. Its author described in non-clerical detail the sensations he experienced when sitting knee-to-knee and toe-to-toe with a young and beautiful woman whose breast and nether limbs he stroked in order to put her into a trance. The anonymous confessor had married the first young lady whose magnetic proximity had caused his most unprofessional thoughts, and during the period of his honeymoon had renounced the black art. But the magnetic fluid was like Concord wine in his veins, and he soon found himself again making the fatal passes and wrecking innumerable marriages, his own first two included.

Since LaRoy Sunderland was at the time the only prominent mesmerist who had been twice divorced, fingers were pointed at him as the author of the *Confessions*. He rushed to press to prove by the bitterness of his denunciations as well as the eloquence of his prose that he could not have written a trashy book. He also felt impelled to challenge to personal debate any Protestant clergyman who accepted the *Confessions* not only as gospel truth but as proof that the magnetic fluid had been brewed by the devil.

A man so well trained in conflict could not accept without quibbling a theory so widespread in its implications as Dr. Buchanan's. Not that Dr. Sunderland questioned the effects the Westerner produced in his subjects; no reasonable man could do so without doubting the evidence of his own eyes. But Dr. Sunderland did quarrel with Buchanan's attempt to make magnetism a subservient science to phrenology and, by tuning up his subjects' organs of susceptibility and then turning them loose, of dispensing with the services of the magnetizer. So LaRoy Sunderland called up his own store of knowledge to invent a counter science in which phrenology would be made subservient to magnetism, and the magnetizer more powerful and indispensable than ever before.

The phrenologist from Kentucky might know his chosen subject perfectly, the magnetizer in New York graciously conceded, but he certainly misunderstood animal magnetism or—as Dr. Sunderland who kept his vocabulary fluid by keeping up with the latest developments in the material sciences, chose to call it—human electricity. Did Dr. Buchanan think that an all merciful Creator—losing his pulpit had not lost Sunderland his ability to talk like an occupant—would allow His children to rush about this earth with nervauric influences shooting out from them like so many comets? Of course He wouldn't. In the human anatomy the electrical impulses were as well regulated as in the material uni-

verse. Didn't the universities at the West teach anything about polarity?

Electrical poles were the real forces behind those
influences that Dr. Buchanan chose to describe as
nervauric. The north poles of the magnetic impulses
were naturally located in the human head; but where
were the south poles anchored? Where else indeed but
in the nearest and handiest place; the human body.
There, said Dr. Sunderland, was the true explanation
of the effects Dr. Buchanan had produced. Every organ
in a man's body had its counterpart somewhere in his
head, either in the phrenological bumps of his skull or
some part of his face. The influences from the bump of
Alimentativeness, for example, flowed directly to the
stomach, those of Veneration to the tendons of the knee-
cap. The organ of Somnolence hooked up with the eyelids; the corners of the lips connected with Mirthful-
ness, their exact center with Amativeness. The positive
pole for each lung was the spot just above the cheek-
bone where the hectic flush spread the romantic banner
of consumption.

LaRoy Sunderland called his theory Pathetism and
he employed it to effect many marvelous and almost
instantaneous cures. By reverse passes on the cheekbones
he caused tubercular patients to cease their coughing
and spitting. With vigorous stimulation of the ankles
he soothed sick headaches. And he cured several men
of intoxication by the negative excitation of one of the
organs of the face, presumably the reddened nose. The

only disease for which he found no corresponding cranial organ was cancer. This did seem to him the one case in which the nervauric influences went unharnessed, spreading their evil helter-skelter throughout the world. So in treating cancer LaRoy Sunderland fell back on Dr. Buchanan's method and effected nice cures by having his patients touch the head of a corpse.

As soon as Dr. Sunderland had his science of Pathetism perfected, he demonstrated its practical superiority over nervaurism before the same commission that had given Dr. Buchanan its scientific O.K.

His subject was another intelligent, blind, afflicted young lady, known to the audience simply as Mary. Before magnetizing her Dr. Sunderland asked a few questions which established her true character. She said that she had been confirmed, thought her pastor the best man on earth, loved her Savior dearly, and hoped to go to Heaven when she died. The preliminaries over, her operator made the necessary passes and placed his hand on Mary's head. From her mouth there came a wail.

She was singing, the beaming Dr. Sunderland reassured the commissioners, because he had just touched her organ of Tune. He then let his finger stray to Self-esteem and Mary stopped her noise, drew herself erect, and said, "I am the greatest person living. I am better than any of you. Yes, indeed, I am."

When the moving finger reached Willfulness her face became sullen and she said in a determined voice, "I will have my way. I will. I will. I will."

When her organs of Language and Causality were aroused together she began to talk a blue streak, beginning every sentence, the scientific gentlemen were pleased to note, with a "Because" or a "Why" or a "Wherefore." When Fear was aroused she cowered back in her chair and whimpered, "Oh, I am afraid. Those gentlemen want to kill me." When Dr. Sunderland tempered her hysteria by touching Reverence slightly she whispered in a low voice, "God is so, so good."

After he had punched all thirty-five major organs, and with the exception of a few minor confusions got the correct responses, her operator was ready for the big surprise of the evening. Quieting Mary—the last organ stimulated had been Love of Approbation, and she was still twisting around and simpering at her audience—he touched with a single mighty stroke Veneration, Worship, Love, Faith, Hope and Adhesiveness, but in a *reverse order.*

Mary shot up from her chair, stood stiff as a ramrod, and pulled her skirts about her so that the gentleman saw there was not even the suggestion of a bend to her knees. "That old pastor at my church," she said, "he thinks he is so much; but me I don't think he's any better than other folks."

"But you love the Savior, don't you, Mary?" her Bergen asked.

Mary tossed her head mockingly and replied, "I don't know as I do."

"And have you no desire to go to Heaven?"

[139]

"I don't care anything about it, and that's the truth," she answered. It was plainly high time for Dr. Sunderland to get her organs of Veneration, Worship, Love, Faith, Hope and Adhesiveness working correctly again, so that her soul would not be damned to eternity.

William Cullen Bryant and his scientific colleagues were profoundly moved by this demonstration, as well they might have been. They had witnessed the miracle of which all reformers dream. They had seen a human being express through her own mouth, with her own voice and gestures, and so far as she knew not against her own will, the sentiments that her manipulator wished her to express. The scientific gentlemen had scientific proof that human nature could be scientifically changed. If it were true that Mary gave the most effective performance when her nature was changed for the worse, then remember, please, with a little tolerance that this was only for the purpose of demonstration. When the science of Pathetism should come into general practical use, it would be employed by benevolent operators only to better the conditions of less fortunate people.

XIII

The Fowlers Explore Love

EVERY LIBERAL FAMILIAR WITH PE-
NOLOGY, TAUTOLOGICALLY SPEAK-
ING, KNOWS FROM HIS FLIGHT FROM
Lombroso that a head, especially if it belongs to a criminal, has virtually nothing to do with the body at all.
For a liberal to admit of a criminal type would be to
admit that he was no liberal. Liberalism has learned
through a peculiarly astral science that one person may
manipulate another—that is reform him. And reform
would be impossible on a type; for the very word car-
ries the connotation of the immutability of Nature's
status quo.

Back in the 1840's, however, it was a practical con-
sideration, not a foreknowledge, that his science would
fall into disrepute among his own kind, that caused
America's greatest phrenologist to add mesmerism to
his other powers. For some years after his triumph as
head of Washington's first real brain trust, Orson
Fowler had been becoming more and more impatient of
Gall's formal classification of the Knowing Sentiments
and those Proper to Man. A familiarity with the locations of Ideality, Benevolence and Sublimity had been

just the ticket when examining the heads of Henry Ward Beecher, Henry Clay and Daniel Webster; but such highfalutin faculties occurred less frequently in the run-of-the-mine customers at the Phrenological Cabinet. Fowler was tremendously impressed therefore when he saw Buchanan and Sunderland, in rummaging through the scalps of their magnetized subjects, apparently hit on organs of which Gall and Spurzheim had been unaware. With the aid of magnetism, and his usual industry and ingenuity, Orson Fowler was soon discovering new faculties that were of real practical help in advising his clients about their personal problems.

He discovered them so rapidly that he was forever having to re-edit his works to make them conform to his reclassifications of the faculties, just as more recent psychologists have been kept perpetually busy revising their textbooks to accommodate their ever-changing lists of instincts. By the time his basic work on phrenology went into its sixty-first edition he had established the existence of eighty-three new organs. And nice homey ones most of them were too; like Money-making, Etiquette, Style, Money-saving, Patriotism, Love of Pets, Love of Keep-sakes, Caressing, Tattling, and Bibation. This last one was pretty inclusive. Bibation not only controlled the desire to drink liquids, but took in washing, bathing, swimming, sailing, and reached out to the arts by disclosing a fondness for seascapes.

The greatest of all his discoveries was the Organ of

Union for Life. He had probably passed his hands over it several thousand times without realizing that it was a distinct bump, for it was in a veritable Alps of the cranium. He might never have found it at all had not a lady, a friend of his wife, complained of an acute headache which afflicted her whenever her husband's business took him away from town. Orson Fowler made passes at one organ after another without relieving her distress. He then suggested that she point out to him the seat of the pain.

Her finger seemed to waver between Amativeness and Adhesiveness, but Mr. Fowler stimulated each of those in turn without producing any change in her condition. But when he very carefully inserted his fingernail between the two, and the lady cried out that the pain had become intense, he knew that he had landed in unexplored territory.

His discovery of Union for Life—which after further research he decided was the organ which purified and refined the sentiment of Love, and gave scientific proof of the well-known fact that woman's affection is more constant than man's—led Orson Fowler to relinquish the greater part of his general practice to his brother Lorenzo. With the competent assistance of Lorenzo's wife, Lydia, a leading figure in the Women's Rights movement, he dedicated more and more of his time and energy to perfecting America's first premarital marriage clinic.

The Fowlers believed in marrying for love—but not

indiscriminately. Too often, they regretted, a young man's organ of Amativeness was aroused by a slender ankle, a soft hand, a small waist or a fine bust. Nothing could be more unfortunate. Unless a youth was quite sure that the bust was the young lady's own, he had best beware, for in these days of padding it was hard to tell a breast from cotton batting; and surely a young woman who would fool a suitor about such things would after marriage deceive him about less protuberant matters. As for soft hands, they necessarily, according to Dr. Sunderland's theory of polarity, accompanied soft brains, just as a small waist accompanied a lack of Philoprogenitiveness, and a slender ankle a brittle heart.

"Marry to suit no one but yourself, not even your parents," Orson Fowler advised his clients, "but allow a phrenologist to guide your choice, for phrenology opens Cupid's eyes and shows how to fall in love intellectually." In general he counseled, "Select as your intended someone whose qualities of intellect and feeling resemble your own, for such a person will most powerfully *excite* and *gratify* your *own* largest organs." But special conditions required more specific recommendations.

A young man whose bump of Acquisitiveness was discovered to be minute was warned, "By no means marry one in whom the organ is also small, lest the combined extravagance of both and the economy of neither bring you to poverty and keep you there." A girl bent on marrying a farmer was urged to bring him to the clinic to have Mr. Fowler pass on the size of his Love of Pets, which would insure his taking good care of his stock, and of his Parental Love which would render him with a disposition eager to improve the breed.

City young people were given a special dissertation on the bump of Inhabitiveness. The universal prevalence of that organ led Orson Fowler to declare that by following the current practice of boarding, renting and annually changing their domiciles, young couples in New York (where he estimated the moving costs on each May 1st to be in excess of $25,000) not only wasted a lot of money, but Violated a Fundamental Law of Nature.

To be sure that she would own her *own* house and garden spot a young woman needed to know more about her intended's Inhabitiveness than that it was large and well developed. She had to have Mr. Fowler's confirmation that the *outer* part of that organ was bigger and better than the inner. Should the reverse be the case, the bride would find herself in a fix, for a husband so afflicted would continue to love, and contribute more generously to, the home of his childhood than any domicile of his own. To be certain that he would never let their house need paint or their garden grow weedy and that he would always buy nice furniture, he needed a big bump of Approbativeness. A young woman so favored could be counted upon to render the home as agreeable as possible.

To all young ladies, whether from town or country, the great phrenologist confided delicately that, like Inhabitiveness, the organ of Amativeness also had two sections. The upper and outer portion which lay close to the ears could be trusted, as it predisposed an unmarried male to nothing more violent than caresses. But the lower and inner parts which manifested mere animal passions—against them a girl must be eternally on guard. Should she by mischance touch that area, even when giving her intended a pure and platonic caress, he would not improbably rob her of her virtue before her wedding morn.

In her "Familiar Lessons on Physiology, Designed for the Use of Children and Youth in Schools and Families," Mrs. Lorenzo Fowler explained Amativeness somewhat differently. It was, she said, the organ which led brother and sister to love each other. Since her brother-in-law had discovered that birds possessed Union for Life, she was able to offer a method for teaching boys and girls the facts about marriage that was so delicate that it did not even offend the parents and teachers who had been outraged at learning that Bronson Alcott dared mention the facts of life at the Temple School.

Though his exploitation of Union for Life added greatly to Orson Fowler's income and his popularity among the Smiths and Joneses, it cost him prestige in the highest intellectual circles. Edgeworth Lazarus was particularly distressed because Fowler's diligent fingers had apparently come upon an anatomical justification of monogamy. Duality in any form, Dr. Lazarus declared, upset the numerical harmony of the celestial spheres. Humanity's perverse and unreasoning tolerance of two-somes had already, he pointed out, produced so much discord as to constitute the earth, which was divinely designed to be a happy planet, a veritable hell. If mankind persisted in following Orson Fowler to its doom, Edgeworth Lazarus could hold out no hope for its eventual redemption.

It was Thomas Nichols who decided the case against Union for Life on more specific grounds. Mr. Nichols had long been impatient of the Fowlers' claims to priority in the bump-feeling field, for while a student at Dartmouth he had started exploring the heads of his classmates two weeks before the skull-rummaging at Amherst had aroused so much attention. He therefore jumped into the present controversy with more vim and venom than Dr. Lazarus. Union for Life could not possibly be a *natural* organ, Thomas Nichols declared, because four-fifths of mankind, including every Turk and most Orientals, lacked it entirely.

"The question of how many other persons one person can love at once," he explained further, "is simply a question of *capacity*. One man is stronger than another; one has greater *versatility*. It is absurd to suppose that no man ever loves more than one wife; as absurd as to suppose that European and American women, as long as they love their husbands, can love nobody else."

Then jumping nimbly from science to ethics, Mr. Nichols finished his argument with this forthright declaration: "I assert that the promise of a man to love any woman as long as he lives is wrong. I denounce, therefore, the civilized marriage as a violation of the laws of nature and the command of God."

No one read these stirring words with greater interest and approval than Mary Gove, now dispensing water cure from a residence on Tenth Street. The months since she came to New York had been busy ones for her.

After living at Bond Street for six weeks she felt that she had absorbed from observing Dr. Shew's practice all that she needed to go into the business for herself. Her funds were still scarce, but on Broadway near Astor Place she found a room that she could afford. It was on the fourth floor of a boardinghouse and so small and inconvenient that the landlady had not been able to rent it. She agreed to let Mrs. Gove and Elma have it, without food, light or heat, for $1.50 a week.

Having been a servant's room in the days when the boardinghouse was a private dwelling, it was dark and cheerless, and 75 cents a week for lamp oil and coal hardly made it livable. But Mrs. Shew contributed bright curtains and the little table that Mrs. Gove had so loved at Bond Street, and Dr. Lazarus the fashionable but incongruous gift of a great flowering rose bush that all but filled the room. Mrs. Gove's recently acquired abhorrence of ordinary food stood her in good stead now. The 25 cents weekly allotment for edibles went into corn meal mush and molasses.

Mrs. Gove was overjoyed soon after she was settled to receive a letter from Mrs. Josepha Hale saying that she was taking three of her stories for *Godey's*. A second letter from the editress, however, contained the hope-dashing information that it would probably be a year before they were published and paid for, and that since Mary Orne—Mrs. Gove's pen name—was unknown to *Godey's* readers the stories would then bring only $5.00 apiece.

Her lack of literary fame brought her the same disappointment when she took the notes of her "Lectures to Ladies" to the Harper brothers. They often paid as much as $10,000 for a book by an eminent author, the head of the firm told her grandly, but until she became well known as a general writer as well as a lecturer to ladies, $100 was the most he could do for her. He did agree to let her have $50 on the spot, the other to be paid when she read the proofs.

With her usual self-confidence she hired a hall, and advertised in the daily papers that the famous Mrs. Gove was resuming in New York the lectures to ladies that had been so well received in Baltimore, Philadelphia, and other leading cities, and that the price for the entire course of twenty lectures would be only $5.00 a lady. Among the thousands of females in the city there must be hundreds sufficiently curious about the workings of their own minds and bodies to insure the instructress a pretty return. Carried away by the prospects, she made arrangements for Elma to take art lessons from the most expensive teacher in town.

The day of the first lecture arrived under bursting clouds. Mrs. Gove, because she had not saved back the three cents for omnibus fare, walked through the rain to the hall, and waited there all afternoon alone. Not a single lady in all New York dared brave the elements even to learn the most startling facts of anatomy, phrenology, magnetism and water cure. Trudging down Broadway at dusk, the bright lights from the oyster bars and the confectioneries showing the ruin of her one new dress, Mary Gove reflected that the apple women shivering in doorways and the sodden newsboys, who would soon crawl back into some filthy rookery at the Five Points, were no poorer than she was.

Back in her cold room she had given in to the novelty of despair and tears when the door opened and Mrs. Shew and Dr. Lazarus came in as merrily as if there had been no fiasco that afternoon. Mrs. Shew had brought her a spring bonnet with violets on it—though Easter was still weeks away—and Dr. Lazarus a solution to her difficulties.

His sister Elena, he told her, was abed with a humor which neither the allopathic medications of Dr. Valentine Mott nor the hydropathic ministrations of Dr. Shew had been able to cure. Neither had transferring her from an old-fashioned school, where she was forced to walk stiffly with her hands clasped over her middle,

to one where she was taught leaping, vaulting and flying in the modern manner, done much good. It was
obvious to her brother that the mental strains and
stresses of an isolate household were getting her down.
Could she be moved to an establishment ruled not by
the unnatural ties of family life but by magnetic affection and humanity love she would, he felt sure, be
soon restored to normal health. Would Mrs. Gove be
willing to preside over such an establishment? Just
would she!

A residence on Tenth Street was procured, an Irish
girl hired, and Mrs. Gove and her daughter, Dr. Lazarus and his sister, along with a congenial group of
refugees from stodgy respectability, moved in. Paren-
thetically, one member of the isolate household who
was left kicking in her crib was little Emma Lazarus
whose lines were to be carved on the Statue of Liberty.

Each guest was allowed to furnish his or her own
bed-chamber; the rest of the house was strictly communal. A kitchen service was installed but seldom used,
because since all the residents were dedicated to the life
of divine-human-individuality, they all held identical
views on the subject of diet and believed that raw food
brought them especially close to the harmonial fountain of Nature. The large parlor—except for the piano-
forte, the forty chairs for Mrs. Gove's lecture audiences
which faced a large unappetizing form upon which she
pointed out those sections peculiarly harassing to females, and enough large and small tables, books, shells,

statuettes, curiosities and keepsakes, to render it cozy—
was left hygienically bare. When the chairs were pushed
to the wall the room was used for gymnastic and cal-
isthentic exercises.

Mrs. Gove was delighted with the people who at
Dr. Lazarus' invitation came to live with them on
Tenth Street. Among them were several philosophers,
two poets, three painters, and a lady who did nothing
but translate the works of George Sand. But no matter
what their vocations, they were all held together by, in
Mary Gove's words, the strong bond of general toleration. Lest someone misunderstand what she meant by
general toleration, she elaborated: "None of us could
know a truth without feeling a compulsion to live and
teach it to *others*." No better definition of tolerance,
as a liberal sees it, has been unearthed to this minute.

The intellectual caliber of this non-isolate group was
so high that Mrs. Gove was able to note with satisfaction that there were only two orthodox Calvinists
among them. She added complacently that one of these
committed suicide; the other went insane. Unfortunately the one who cracked directed the malignant attraction of his darkening soul upon the budding Elma
in a manner not gleaned from the teachings of John
Calvin. Mary Gove, for all her toleration, could not
reconcile that state of affairs with the noble designs of
Nature. She agreed regretfully that the girl should be
returned to New Hampshire.

Under the eager questioning of her backwoods relatives, Elma described the goings-on at her mother's residence in graphic detail—so graphic indeed that they led Hiram Gove to announce flatly to his delighted neighbors that his wife was down in New York running a bawdy house.

When news of this black-hearted calumny reached Mary Gove she exclaimed, "I do not say God forgive him!—there are sins for which we cannot pray." And getting down to earth, she countered prettily, "But if I had kept a house of infamy, I would not have let *him* in."

XIV

Mr. Poe Introduces Mrs. Gove
to the Intelligentsia

MRS. HIRAM GOVE IN NEW YORK DID
INDEED HAVE LITTLE TIME TO
BOTHER OVER RUSTIC HIRAM. HER
mind, bee that it was, had fastened on more interesting
and profitable matters. Besides her instructions to ladies
in the Tenth Street parlor, she was carrying on a brisk
hydropathic business by mail. But not all her literary
ability was drained off in prescribing letters.

Besides her novels and the stories she contributed to
Godey's and the *Broadway Journal,* she wrote articles
on phrenology, magnetism and corsetless-dressing for
Dr. Shew's *Herald of Reform* and other radical journals. She also did the water cure column for the conservative *Whig Review.* One day its editor, George
Hooker Colton, took her by way of the Harlem Railroad on a little jaunt into the country to meet another
contributor of his, Edgar Allan Poe.

Of all the literary ladies who flocked to Fordham to
worship the author of "The Raven," only Mary Gove
was more impressed by the actual human drama oc-
curring in that bare neat cottage under the cherry trees

than by the rehearsed histrionics of the celebrated poem. Poe discussed with her as with the others authorship and fame, but she learned to know him best as the gentle nephew and son-in-law of stalwart, patient Mrs. Clemm. Mrs. Gove was thus the only one of the literary ladies who noted the homey details of that strangely devoted family group, details which realistic biographers, groping through the odorous mist that Griswold spread over his corpse, have needed to get a recognizable picture of the man. It is from her *Reminiscences of Edgar Allan Poe* that the biographers— and the Broadway playwrights, Hollywood scenarists, and radio dramatists—have taken the props which are now so familiar: the checked matting, the letter from Elizabeth Barrett, the burst gaiters, the immaculate sheets on the blanketless straw, the West Point coat and the great cat serving as cover for the dying Virginia.

These reminiscences Mary Gove set down years later in London; at the time she was more interested in doing something to relieve the poverty. Her first thought was of the man who had detected in Poe as well as herself the particular talents that were to bring them fame. She wrote to John Neal and asked him to get Poe some paying work. But in the years since the unknown poet had inscribed his first thin volume to the American who had just been acclaimed to international stature by the English, and Neal had deserted realistic fiction for the superman strip of Liberalism, the early mutual admiration had changed to intellectual distrust. Brother Jonathan wa'n't to home.

Mary Gove turned next to a friend whose mere identity was destined to confound every biographer of Poe. Marie Louise Shew, not unaware of the drama in the poet's plight, excitedly dispatched a feather bed, along with plentiful bed clothing and other comforts, to Fordham, followed the next week by a purse of $60. From then on she kept a watchful eye on the stricken cottage and on Poe when he was in the city.

In his *Doings of Gotham* Poe had written, "Some person, falling from the roof of a house, and receiving severe injury, has been wrapped up by somebody else in a wet sheet, and not immediately dying in consequence but getting well in spite of the sheets, somebody else again has written a letter to the *Tribune* extolling the 'Hydropathy' or water cure of that monarch of charlatans, Priessnitz. Whereupon, all the medical world of Gotham are by their ears . . ."

Mrs. Shew knew, if Poe did not, that the "somebody else" and the "somebody else again" were both the same somebody, her husband Joel Shew, but she was too sure of her good works to be restrained by any mockery of her science. And when Poe was loose on the town she often sheltered him at 47 Bond Street. There he stayed, eating if not his words at least a Priessnitzian diet, until his hangover was spent. In the conservatory directly under Mrs. Gove's old room he was driven to "The Bells" by the clangs from the nearby nest of churches.

Mr. Poe Introduces Mrs. Gove

To further her own ministrations Mrs. Shew at times called in the celebrated Doctors Francis and Mott for the unstrung poet. Valentine Mott's assertion that continued use of stimulants by his patient would be fatal has been the cornerstone of all the stories that Poe was a drug addict. It has gone unnoted that the doctor's words were set down by Mrs. Shew, and that to a water curist "Stimulants" meant coffee, condiments and tea, with no thought of opiates.

Do-gooder that she was, Mrs. Shew was not above looking out for her own material interests. When the unmanageable Mr. Poe began gumming up her pre-divorce efforts to land a wealthy second husband, she cut the friendship decisively.

By then her frequent excursions to Fordham had brought some happy changes into Mary Gove's life. Knowing Poe had made her a member of the top flight literary set in New York to which his imaginative pen was each month giving glamour in the *Ladies' Book* under the title he had thought up for them—the Literati.

When Poe in 1844 moved from Philadelphia to New York, and found most of his fellow writers already there, he arranged with Louis Godey to do a series of sketches about them, paying especial attention to those features of the great ones in which the public would be sure to have the most interest—their phrenological developments. What might have been a tough assignment for Poe became easy when in launching his short-lived

Broadway Journal he rented floor space in Clinton Hall from the Fowlers, and could thus look at their Cabinet whenever he wanted to.

The New York Literati series was an instant success. Mr. Godey had often to get out three extra editions of those numbers of his magazine in which the profiles appeared in order to satisfy his readers' curiosity about the private lives of their favorite writers. So that they might learn, for example, that the authors of the most beloved poems—George Morris who wrote "Woodman, Spare That Tree," Mrs. Josepha Hale who did "Mary Had a Little Lamb," and Robert Dunne English who had hit the jack-pot with "Ben Bolt"—were in their less rhythmical moments hard working editors. That Fitz-Greene Halleck got the leisure to write *his* poems—which, though they received high praise from his fellow writers, nobody else liked or understood—by serving as confidential clerk to unlettered old Mr. Astor. That Dr. Francis, besides being New York's most expensive obstetrician, displayed when out of ear-shot of the ladies a wit reminiscent of Benjamin Franklin. That his rival at repartee, Professor George Bush of the Union Theological Seminary, the recognized authority upon the Resurrection, the Millennium, Mohammedanism, and the fundamental spiritual affinity between Mesmer and Swedenborg, looked and had manners exactly like old man Biddle. That Laughton Osborn, who had shocked those who could afford to buy his esoterica by questioning Colonel Stone's motives for investigating the sleeping cells of the Montreal nuns, and by describing Miss Brackett as "floating about in a seminal state," was not only one of the richest but most charming play-boys in New York. That pretty Mrs. Frances Osgood cared more about making others happy through her songs than in gaining the fame that would establish her as an authority upon etiquette, handiwork and cookery. That Nathaniel Willis had perfect teeth and never required waving tongs because his hair curled naturally. That on Mrs. Cora Mowatt even the hydropathic head-dress looked smart.

Three months after she was received into this charmed and envied group a busy lady on Tenth Street was gratified to read the following in the column in the *Lady's Book* signed "E.A.P.":

"Mrs. Mary Gove, under the pseudonym of 'Mary Orne,' has written many excellent papers for the magazines. Her subjects are usually tinctured with the mysticism of the transcendentalists, but are truly imaginative. Her style is quite remarkable for its luminousness and precision—two qualities very rare in her sex. An article entitled 'The Gift of Prophecy,' published in the *Broadway Journal*, is a fine specimen of her manner.

"Mrs. Gove, however, has acquired less notoriety by her literary compositions than by her lectures on physiology to classes of females. These lectures are said to have been instructive and useful; they certainly elicited much attention. Mrs. Gove has also given public discourses on Mesmerism, I believe, and other similar themes—matters which put to the severest test the credulity or, more properly, the faith of mankind. She is, I think, a Mesmerist, a Swedenborgian, a phrenologist, a homeopathist, and a disciple of Priessnitz—more I am not prepared to say.

"She is rather below medium height, somewhat thin, with dark hair and keen, intelligent black eyes. She converses well and with enthusiasm. In many respects a very interesting woman."

This write-up not only brought to Mary Gove the fame after which she had been hankering, but invitations to the social functions of the Literati—activities that were so constantly and fulsomely described by their participants in all the leading magazines that they became the models of entertaining from Rittenhouse Square to the cottages along the Wabash.

Though a few dansantes were held in the afternoon, most of the parties occurred after supper and lasted till well after midnight, when light refreshments—ice-cream, jelly, small cakes, comfits, wine, nuts and raisins —were served. The soft glow of candles was preferred to the more brilliant gas light. There was always violin or piano music for those who wished to dance; and witty entertainment in which everyone present participated.

The game of Twenty Questions was especially favored by those with strong magnetic powers. Mrs. Osgood thought up the idea of having each guest write a mimic letter from some impossible hero or lion excusing himself from accepting an invitation—for instance, Boz must send regrets for his followers would not approve his attending any function as the escort of George Sand. Finally, when Miss Charlotte Lynch introduced charades at one of her soirées and had dignified philosophers and aloof poets cavorting all over the place, Mrs. Shew remarked, "La, I should think we should call them Algonquins after those wild Indians that used to be hereabout."

But life among the intelligentsia was not, in Mrs. Gove's phrase, entirely conundrums and comfits. Even when the piano tinkled most merrily and the jelly shimmered at its brightest, poems and essays were read aloud and serious conversations engaged in. Once at every gathering Poe would be asked to recite "The Raven." As soon as the last "Nevermore" had rolled off his tongue, the hostess would quickly light more candles and all the gas jets, the musicians would raise a loud Ethiopian tune, and all the guests would dance madly. This antidote was necessary to restore the spirits of the ladies. If they went home with the raven's prophesy still croaking in their ears, they would be depressed for days.

The December after Mrs. Gove joined the Literati Mrs. Osgood, who was suffering an inflammation of the lungs, came to spend a few weeks with her in order to enjoy, in addition to her companionship, the benefits of water cure. Seeing how large the parlors were, Mrs. Osgood suggested that they throw a Christmas party.

Seventy ladies and gentlemen, she reckoned, could stand and move easily about the premises. Since the Literati proper comprised no more than half this number, Mrs. Gove asked whom else they should invite.

To which Mrs. Osgood replied, "All the editors who are not yet frozen into their dignity and dullness; all the poets who have genius and reputation in embryo; all the artists who are ordained such, though they may not have made their calling and election sure; pretty girls for wall flowers; and any literary woman, of decided talent, who wears clean gloves and whole hose."

Mrs. Gove was thrilled but appalled by the idea. She confessed to Mrs. Osgood that, in the Fourieristic phrase, she was probably as big a fool as the climate allowed of, but she would have no idea how to manage so large an affair. There had been no music and dancing and the paying of pretty compliments in Goffstown, New Hampshire.

Two years' residence in London—while her husband executed the commissions which his portrait of Harriet Martineau had secured him—had given Mrs. Osgood an enviable standing among the matrons of New York. She told her hostess not to worry. All she need do was provide the parlors, a good fire and plenty of light; Mrs. Osgood would take care of the rest.

Christmas gifts, she suggested, could be poems and articles written by the guests. She would herself compose a comic song for the occasion, which she could probably sell afterwards to the *Ladies' Companion*, of which she was an editress, for $10. And Mr. Poe would surely contribute an original poem, she reminded Mrs. Gove with pardonable smugness, remembering the flutter that had been occasioned at Miss Lynch's Valentine Party the spring before by the acrostic he dedicated to Frances Osgood. They could, of course, count on wealthy Albert Brisbane for the refreshments and the music. But even if he did raise an orchestra, she was still going to preside at the pianoforte, Mrs. Osgood said firmly, in order to break in when the festivities grew dull. If she didn't then Cora Mowatt would certainly—to use a word which had become conversationally *de rigeur* among the younger contributors to the *Lady's Book* since Mrs. Hale forebade them to write it—"hog" the whole period assigned to the recitations.

They were busy with the preparations—Mrs. Osgood supplying the fashionable rustic touch, which Thoreau was apotheosizing at Walden, by fashioning candle-holders from potatoes—when Mrs. Gove referred again to the splendor of Thomas Nichols' stand against the existence of the organ of Union for Life. "That gentleman," she confided, "discovers my own secret thoughts. Though we have never met, I feel we must share strong attractional bonds."

Mrs. Osgood did not immediately reply, but turned upon her companion her sunniest smile in which a touch of mischief lurked. That evening as the two ladies were putting their hair into curl papers against the festivities of the morrow, the teasing expression returned to

[163]

Frances Osgood's lips. "I have bagged your paragon," she said.

Mary Gove's heart began to flutter and it continued to flutter until the moment the next evening when she spied her paragon; and then it sank. Thomas Nichols arrived at the party accompanied by Albert Brisbane; and the contrast between the two was overwhelming.

Tall, pale Brisbane, with his massive forehead, graceful hands, intense perforating eyes, halting speech and jerky gestures, looked, as everyone who knew him agreed in admiration, the perfect radical. Consequently even on Christmas he dressed the part, with his clothes mussed, his collar open à la Byron, and his hair long. But Mr. Nichols wore a stiff white waistcoat, gleaming white gloves, and a coat of faultless Parisian fit. As Mrs. Osgood presented him to Mrs. Gove, he bowed stiffly from the waist and said, "Madame, will you pardon a busy man for being kept out of Paradise much longer than he wished or intended to be?"

Mary Gove in disappointed sorrow felt compelled secretly to apply to him her most abhorred adjectives: staid, allopathic and conservative. But as he talked longer this impression vanished. They had, they discovered, been born within two years and fifty miles of one another, but they did not waste precious minutes recalling mutual friends in bleak, pious New Hampshire. They had more vital bonds in common.

Like Mary Gove, Thomas Nichols had from childhood felt an urge to serve his fellowmen by teaching

them the proper way to live. To that end he had gone
to Dartmouth to study medicine. But listening to one
lecture by Sylvester Graham had shown him how false
was the art of healing as taught in most colleges in the
1830's. So dropping his studies he came to New York
where Bennett engaged him as editor of the *Evening
Herald*.

The chief's insistence that he give more attention to
the balls and receptions of the Brevoorts and the Liv-
ingstons than to the lectures of the intellectuals had
irked him for a while but within two years he had gathered enough material about the manners and morals of
the Nabobs of Washington Square to write two successful novels of society life. Nor had he let these activities divert him from his original ambition. While
he observed the fashionables he also studied phrenology, mesmerism and the other sciences. Though he
looked more the dandy than Nat Willis, he was a more
zealous reformer than even Brisbane. In Buffalo where
he had gone to work for the *Commercial Advertiser*,
he had so ardently exposed the morals of the political
bosses of the town that he got slapped into prison for
libel. His reminiscences of four months in the Erie
jail were of great interest to Mrs. Gove for such institutions had been suggested as suitable for her more
than once.

XV

Stardust in Their Eyes

IN LOOKING BACK UPON HIS FIRST MOMENTOUS MEETING WITH MARY GOVE, WHEN THE MINGLED RAYS OF wisdom and love broke with a blinding new light upon him, Thomas Nichols was wont to recall, "My destiny was immediately joined to hers, in the holiest of bonds; and our studies and work, as well as our lives, lay henceforth in the same track."

Actually these two impassioned souls could not be immediately joined in the holiest of bonds for the annoying reason that Mr. Nichols had also left an unloved spouse in New Hampshire. Mrs. Gove was such an ardent convert to his disbelief in monogamy that she was eager to live with him without bothering about the formality of divorce, until she discovered that although the laws of God were still as high as the heavens above those made by man, there was one of mortal manufacture on the statute books of New Hampshire which would enable Hiram to jail her if she lived openly with Mr. Nichols in the love nest he was preparing. For once discretion seemed even to her not completely unwise.

[166]

Stardust in Their Eyes

While awaiting their legal freedom, Thomas Nichols put in his time in a way that was of great future benefit both to himself and to his affianced. He had perceived immediately that the lack of an academic degree had deprived her, despite her high scientific attainments, of proper recognition in the highest medical circles. Her sex still barred her from all native universities, but her beloved saw a way to get around that difficulty. *He* could obtain the degree and share it with her after their marriage as Joel Shew was sharing his with Marie Louise.

As Thomas Nichols was at this time "fortunately unemployed," he enrolled as a full-time student at the University of New York. After attending the requisite 500 lectures and cliniques under Valentine Mott and his allopathic colleagues—and having many a good smile to himself over the thought of the revolutionary purposes to which he was going to put the reactionary knowledge they dispensed—he graduated near the head of his class.

In the meanwhile, a decided change was coming over the hydropathic columns of the *Whig Review.* Smack in the middle of advice about applying water for colic and measles there would appear learned discourses on derangements of the seasons, fraud, the isolate household, poverty, and the individualization of the divine dynamic principles—topics which seemed to have little bearing on the specific malady being prescribed for.

The proprietor of the journal complained to Colton,

who in turn reproved Mrs. Gove. "People are beginning to think well of you as a physician," he told her. "That last cure of croup, wherein you keep the infant's feet continuously in cold water, did you great credit. But you had best leave the discussion of the more radical problems to the men." He finished with the hint that if she didn't he would be looking around for another health editor.

To which Mary Gove retorted with conviction, if not pertinence, "My haven is the broad ocean of harmony of the future, where freedom shall take the place of bonds, where all shall follow attraction as unerringly as the planets move about the sun." From which Colton knew that with Thomas Nichols' persuasion added to Edgeworth Lazarus' original influence, she had augmented her other credos with a glowing belief in the philosophy of Fourier as propounded in this country by Albert Brisbane.

Following the example set by such wealthy young men as Nicholas Biddle and Henry Calvert, Brisbane had gone to Europe, engaged an English-speaking tutor, and begun to dabble with any profound idea that struck his fancy. He had already visited Hegel in Berlin, where he found the intellectual atmosphere particularly congenial, and had mastered animal magnetism to the point where his bare fingers had become more efficacious than flint for lighting his gas jet, when he met the man who changed his life.

Charles Fourier, when Brisbane came across him, was

a middle-aged clerk employed in the Paris office of an American firm. He had got stardust in his eyes much earlier, for he came to maturity in Lyons when the members of the Society of Harmony, forbidden to practice mesmerism in France, had established that city as the capital cell from which to set the magnetic fluid flowing again across the Continent. Fourier thought up finer things to do with the astral influence than use it simply to titillate the most dissolute group of a dying aristocracy. He planned to employ it for exorcising all the social evils which that devastating and voracious monster known as "modern civilization" had visited upon the world; and, if need be, for changing the very make-up of the universe.

Though with the same thoroughness he applied to the accounts of his American employers, Fourier had worked out the most minute detail of his social-astral re-organization plan, not more than ten persons who had read his treatise on Associationism could understand it at all. Brisbane took what the French called Fourier's "unintelligibility" as a challenge, and offered to pay the clerk five francs a lesson to explain his ideas to him from a to izzard.

He had completed his twelfth lesson when mental prostration induced by the intense concentration and bad air, befouled by materialistic Parisian thoughts, forced his return to America. Fourier's teachings—with their strange concepts of attraction, series, cosmic harmony, and planetary subversive action—were still pretty confused in his mind when he embarked. But the rhythm of the steamship and the pure atmosphere of the Atlantic, virgin to contaminated thinking, cleared his brain and restored its natural vigor. By the time the boat docked at New York a great vision floated before his mind. Describing the experience, as he did hundreds of times in subsequent years, he said:

"Far away in the distant future I saw a globe resplendently cultivated and embellished, transformed into the grandest and most beautiful work of art by the combined efforts of all humanity. I saw a race developed, perfected by the continued influence, generation after generation, of true social institutions; a humanity worthy of that Cosmic Soul of which I instinctively felt it to be a part. I saw this resplendent humanity as a child of God, a god itself upon its planet; and the old intuition which had led me to combat the cold atheism of my father was now becoming clearer."

He also saw that he need no longer worry about emulating the old man and becoming a personal success. He could now dedicate his talents, his very life, to the service of all humanity; and he could try to formulate what he could remember of Fourier's ideas into a practical plan for reformation, first of America and then of the human race.

He found America already growing sympathetic toward reform. The ideas of the abolitionists, the total abstinence folk and the anti-rent crowd, were progressing rapidly from the dreams of a few radicals to hard-headed political movements. Viewed against his own great vision, such "fragmentary" strivings seemed "frivolous." Somewhat more serious was the financial depression that was gripping the country, brought on by the failure of the Bank of the United States and the resultant crashing of the New York Stock Exchange.

Though he feared that with his health so impaired by all the thoughts he had forced upon his young mind he might need a full four years to complete his over-all plan for solving permanently all the political, social and climatic problems of America, Brisbane was sure that he could clean up this secondary economic problem in a few months if he could only get the willing co-operation of his erstwhile fellow countrymen. He summoned the employees on his father's estate near Batavia and the local tradesmen to a conference.

There was talk in Washington, he reminded them, of issuing specie, a very reactionary and piecemeal expedient. Instead of providing the banks with new currency the government should take from them whatever notes, and gold and silver too, they still had left. Having destroyed the undemocratic power of the bankers the government could then destroy that of the businessmen by persuading the farmers and other workers to stop *selling* their products, and store them for equitable distribution in vast government-owned ever-normal depots. In conclusion, Mr. Brisbane told his fellow conferees that he would be willing to go to Albany and lay their plan for economic re-organiaztion before the legislature.

The Brisbane name commanded almost as much respect on the Hudson as in the lake country, and the young enthusiast was invited to address the Senate—and got the first of the disillusionments that were to dog his career. Only a single Senator could even comprehend his self-evident principle. The rest pronounced it visionary, and refused either to enact it into law or to recommend it to President Jackson.

Though saddened to find so-called practical men so stupid, Brisbane was not particularly discouraged. After all, this currency theory was but a mere detail in the great work to which he had dedicated himself—that of presenting to the American people a well-rounded plan for their complete social re-organization and spiritual redemption.

He was going to make his fellow citizens truly free. Not promise them superficial and trivial rights like those mentioned in the Declaration of Independence, but emancipate them for good and at one whack from all the social and metaphysical evils of non-Fourieristic civilization. To do so he would first demolish all political boundaries—those which isolated cities, townships and private families, as well as states and nations. Then everyone would be repopulated in specially constructed, self-sustaining, co-operative phalansteries; for only in a community organized and governed by the exact rules laid down by the Fourier could men attain true freedom.

In each community—which would be replete with every commodity essential to successful living, including central heating, bathrooms, supervised playgrounds, nursery schools, and a continuous round of lectures, operas, calisthenic exercises, theatrical performances, orchestral concerts and communal dances—everyone would practice those skills in which he desired to be proficient. Women would be given special opportunities for discovering their true aptitudes, for while they could produce all the children they wished, they would never have to tend them. All other disagreeable tasks would take care of themselves, too, for as soon as the communal soul thrust through the darkness of civilization, men and women would "always *want* to do only those things which they *should* do."

Thus within a phalanx governed by the ideas of Fourier all the problems that misguided leaders sought to solve by wars and laws would disappear. Selfishness would go and with it poverty, malnutrition, evil, improper housing, idleness, error, unhappiness, sickness and prejudice. Everyone would become healthy, prosperous and at peace. Love and trust would take the place of suspicions and duplicity in the relationships of mankind.

The associations would multiply and the aura of beneficence spreading out before them would change even the face of nature. Inclement regions could not withstand the thin layer of air encircling the globe, happily laden with the exhalations of a joyous humanity. The breaths of the phalansterists would transform deserts into cool gardens and arctic wastes into lush orange groves. As the need for more land arose, the seas would respond to benevolent barometry; they would dwindle to mere lakes and their contents, perchance, to lemonade. Soon the entire globe from pole to pole would be crowded with millions of phalanxes and room required for more. By then communication with the other planets would be possible, and through such communications it would be simple to remove the surplus inhabitants of the earth to other whirling spheres. Then the entire cosmos would lay revealed and accessible to man—and man would really begin to go places.

To show that such a plan was not only practical and fool-proof, but rendered all business matters self-evident and easy, and admitted of neither quarrels nor misunderstandings, Brisbane drew up this model of an individual's relation to his association during one year:

Account of J. Jones with the North American Phalanx
Debits:

For rent of rooms	$200.00
Board	175.00
Wearing apparel	150.00
Articles purchased	250.00
Subscription to library, concerts, baths, etc.	25.00
Cash advanced	250.00
Sundries	50.00
Total debts	$1100.00

Credits:

By interest in stock	$400.00
Share of profits in works of Necessity	400.00
Share of profits in works of Usefulness	300.00
Share of profits in works of Attractiveness	200.00
Total credits	$1300.00
Balance	$200.00

When his five years of cogitation were up, Brisbane decided it was time to share the results with his fellow Americans. He moved to New York City and rented a large room at the busy corner of Broadway and Canal Street as the proper setting for writing the monumental work which he planned to call simply *Brisbane on Association*. But like many another thinker, he discovered that the lofty ideas that seemed so illuminating when he just thought them, or repeated them to his friends, lacked, when set down on paper, a certain cohesion that the printer required before transmitting them to type. Brisbane wanted editorial help and, needing the best, he hired Parke Benjamin.

One afternoon as the two were reading proof, Benjamin laughed. "You know," he said to his astonished employer, "Horace Greeley is just damned fool enough to believe such nonsense?"

"And who," asked Mr. Brisbane, "is Mr. Greeley?"

"Oh," said Benjamin, "he's that young man upstairs who edits the *New-Yorker*."

With that Brisbane gathered up a fistful of proofs, and leaping up the stairs, thrust them into the disjointed and reluctant hands of a little bald-headed man. He was extremely busy, Greeley informed his impetuous visitor, making plans for a daily newspaper. In fact this very night he was leaving for Boston to engage some of the finest literary talent in New England to write for him. On Brisbane's insistence, however, he agreed to take the pages with him and if he had time read them on the train.

Two days later it was Horace Greeley who burst unannounced into Albert Brisbane's room. "Only thus," he exclaimed, waving the now much-read proofs under their author's nose, "can the miseries and suffering of the lower classes be alleviated." Then reducing the principles of Attractive Industry to its ultimate simplicity, and a hominess that Brisbane had not suspected it possessed, he said, "Here is a woman who does not know how to keep house . . . let us then organize a system of living that will dispense with the labors of four-fifths of the women now engaged in the kitchen."

So close was the bond of understanding between these two young men—the son of a fabulously wealthy landowner and the boy from a barren New Hampshire farm —that Brisbane took a column in the *Tribune* to explain his ideas to the public. He thus started the tradition of the personal column which his son developed to the lushness of our day. But there was more than one striking difference between the columning of the two Brisbanes: it was not in San Simeon hay that Arthur was paid, while Albert shelled out real money to Greeley for his allotted space.

XVI
Albert Brisbane and His New Order

BEING AN OLD NEWSPAPERMAN PROVED SO CONGENIAL TO ALBERT BRISBANE THAT AS QUICKLY AS HE could, he bought in a half dozen sheets for himself; and hired Osborne MacDaniel and William Henry Channing to help Parke Benjamin edit them for him. Thus fate had it that the three men whose pens did most to spread Fourier's vision of a new transplendent humanity should be the very same trio that spread the glad tidings of Professor Ives' resurrection from Dr. Shew's dripping sheets. They were fast becoming the magi of the new sciences.

William Watson Webb, however, did not find the new order as congenial to his disposition as cold water. He made fun of it. Brisbane was sure that this levity was attributable entirely to ignorance. So each time that he would read in the *Courier and Enquirer* a particularly sarcastical comment on his latest pronouncements, he would go around to see his fellow editor and explain in person exactly what he had meant to say in print. Colonel Webb would take careful notes of the interview and publish them verbatim in his next edition. And to Albert Brisbane's perpetual surprise, his own words set down in the Tory columns of the *Courier*, against the latest reports on the stock market in New York and the grain market in London, looked sillier than ever.

No spirit of levity, however, marred his relations with the New England intellectuals. As soon as he learned through Greeley that the most highly regarded of them were now living—the heartiest among them the year round, the more squeamish on week-ends and vacations—on their communal acres near West Roxbury, he sent Channing and several of his most able agents to show them how to convert their subsistence homestead into a true phalanx. Brook Farm right away took on new life, breadth and elevation.

Brisbane's propagandists taught the farmers how to become Fourieristically self-sustaining by ceasing to sell their surplus agricultural products in Boston. They taught them how, by properly understanding and developing their natural passions, they would come to enjoy work that was necessary, like dish-washing and gardening, as much as that which like writing and talking was merely attractive. So successful was the experiment that when a few months later Brisbane went up to inspect it and George Ripley took him to the kitchen where poets, professors and lecturers were happily peeling potatoes, shelling peas, scouring pots and collecting slops for the hogs, he exclaimed, "What a cathedral of the mind!"

Back in New York Brisbane quickly trained more

propagandists whom he took with him when he expounded his ideas in other progressive centers of the country—Harrisburg, Cincinnati, Louisville, and wherever the interest in his ideas warranted. At his lectures the enthusiasm whipped up by his stooges soon spread to the audiences. Whenever a handful of men caught the spirit simultaneously they would quit their jobs, sell their belongings, pile their families and whatever furniture was left into a wagon, invest their combined money in a piece of land that was cheap, usually because it was not tillable, and set up a phalanx. Soon there were more than forty in the United States.

All except Brook Farm were a bitter disappointment to their inspirer. Hopefully he inspected one after the other, expecting to find them populated by true idealists like himself. Instead he encountered men and women whom he described as visionaries, fanatics, idlers, escapists, non-conformists, and men without industrial aptitudes or any grasp of practical affairs. The North American Phalanx in New Jersey was the one exception. It was inhabited by honest workingmen, who just to be on the safe side kept their jobs in the mills and factories of this imperfect world while preparing themselves for the greater glories that were to come.

Horace Greeley found the North American Phalanx a true inspiration and spent many happy week-ends there dispensing culture to the inmates. Brisbane admitted that the North Americans had a great deal of social intercourse which they seemed to enjoy, but for

[179]

himself he found them as uncouth and uncharming as any other members of the "industrial classes." The North American Phalanx had one great distinction: it lasted twelve years, while most of the others folded up in half that many months.

The collapse of Brook Farm was considered a happy circumstance, for it allowed Ripley, Charles W. Dana and the most rabidly Fourieristic of the homesteaders to move to New York, whence Margaret Fuller had already preceded them. There, while sustaining themselves by reviewing books for the Sunday *Tribune*, they could devote the time which at West Roxbury they had been obliged to spend on the pigs and cows, to working out the details of the new order with Greeley and Brisbane.

There would have been nothing for the inhabitants of the other flopping phalansteries to do on the *Tribune* even had they been able to thumb a ride to New York. And as Albert Brisbane saw these less literate associations disbanding almost as rapidly as they formed— their members homeless, jobless, and with all their possessions gone—he became "deeply impressed with the evils of a too-hasty propaganda." All in all, he thought he had better taken another trip to France and try to discover what had gone wrong.

Fourier was dead by then but had left behind a pile of manuscript which none of his countrymen could read. His American disciple acquired all rights to it easily, and within two years had not only read but sorted it.

He then began to sum up and take an inventory of what he knew. He made a stunning discovery. In his earlier concentration upon self-evident cosmic principles he had overlooked several practical details which now loomed large in his summary, and readily explained the failure of the American experiments. According to Fourier's estimates a single association to have a fair chance of survival required an assemblage of 1,800 people carefully selected from every social class, a fertile acreage of three square miles, and an initial outlay of not less than $500,000.

The shock of this discovery would have fazed a less idealistic person than Albert Brisbane. He, on the other hand, instead of sitting on his intellectual haunches to wait for the number of necessary people, acres and dollars to accumulate, launched into his most sustained flight of planning and thinking into the future. He talked so earnestly and so tirelessly about that great day when all would follow attraction as unerringly as the planets move about the sun, that his friends and admirers were quite certain that he was possessed by the soul of Fourier, just as all well informed persons knew that Andrew Jackson Davis had become the earthly mouthpiece of the celestial Swedenborg.

In the most select intellectual gathering places in New York, and especially at the Lazarus-Gove establishment on Tenth Street, endless and animated discussions of the great plan took place. Just where, for example, within the three square miles of a phalanx should the manor house—which would contain the library, the theater, the scientific nursery, the opera, the concert and dancing rooms, and the baths—be located so that everyone of the 1,800 inhabitants could reach it at the same time? Awaiting the day when beneficent exhalations had done away with inclement weather, how could things be so arranged that no one—not even those assigned to work in the fields—got wet during rainy spells? By what means should the various phalanxes communicate with each other? Gigantic signal towers on the manor houses were considered more practical than mail service or the magnetic telegraph, because they would serve equally well when contact was made with the other planets whose inhabitants, perchance, had neither post nor telegraph offices. More important still, where should the central phalanx be located? Some thought Lyons out of deference to Fourier; others stuck out for Bethlehem, Judea, or Batavia, New York, for those little towns had produced great men too; a few thought it would be best to stay the final decision until interplanetary contact was made; but most agreed on Constantinople, because the Turks of all the peoples of this earth had best resisted that arch-curse of mankind —modern civilization.

Of all the discussions those concerning the vestels and vestales and the sacred legions caused the most heated arguments. The great question in regard to the vestales and vestels was this: how long should they rigorously preserve their virginity, and how could they,

without coercion, be made to want to do so? To receive
the highest honors and be made the idols of the phalanx
seemed to Albert Brisbane the proper compensation for
physical intactness until the eighteenth year. Eyes were
lifted at Mary Gove and Thomas Nichols when that
pair doubted if it would work unless the age limit was
drastically reduced.

Sacred Legion was the name for those who would
have to assume the performance of uncleanly and re-
pulsive works and functions, which, alas, humanity still
being unperfected, would have to be countenanced in
the first phalanxes. Realistic individuals contended that
such duties presented no problem to the principles of
Attractive Industry. Simply turn them over to boys between the ages of nine and fifteen who, as everyone
knew, were filthy brats. They had no natural antipathy
toward dirty and offensive contacts, but a positive taste
for them. They would love the job.

The more idealistic thought otherwise. Admission to
the Sacred Legion, they said, must be made so difficult
that it would become a signal honor. Then its members
would execute their duties not from a depraved sense
of pleasure but from generous and noble sentiments and
motives. They would tend the communal offal in the
same high-minded manner as the abstaining youths
would their individual virtue.

Laughton Osborn, happening in on a party where
such discussions had grown particularly impassioned,
suggested that in a completely harmonious universe

the earth's orbit should be slightly slanted in order to conform to the well-known anatomical peculiarities of Far Eastern women. Albert Brisbane said there was no sense to the suggestion, that Fourier had made no plans for such a biased contingency, and that, perhaps, Mr. Osborne was indulging in his habitual and anti-social vice of frivolity.

When Brisbane became particularly inspired he could, so it was claimed, discourse on the new order for from ten to thirty hours without respite. Such intense concentration inevitably told upon his health, and he was again threatened with nervous prostration. Learning that a revolution had dethroned Louis Phillipe and restored a Napoleon in his place, Brisbane figured that the intellectual atmosphere of Paris must thereby have become more healthful, for Bonaparte was said to have been an admiring student of Fourierism by no less an authority on that subject than Charles Fourier himself.

So in 1848 Albert Brisbane sailed once more for France, and heard upon disembarking that there was at the moment leading a labor disturbance in Cologne a thirty-year-old agitator whose theories of social reorganization were considered by some socialists to be more practical than Fourier's. Brisbane hastened to Germany; but he saw in Karl Marx nothing but a stubborn, stockily built, bushy-haired labor leader.

Marx's hatred of capitalism was so great, Brisbane learned in his first conversation with him, that he was intent on destroying the system right away—instead of, according to Fourier's wiser counsel, seizing it as the spoils upon which to build the better world of the future. Moreover, Marx believed that a new order could be posited on a purely economic upset; he had not the "genius" to comprehend that true socialism must be "the science of instincts and intuitions." Marxianism, Brisbane was sure, would not outlive its originator, and held no interest at all for "educated people."

Albert Brisbane gladly left Karl Marx to his labor-mongering and returned to New York to attest the brighter vision of the Sage of Hyde Park. The Sage was the ultimate, and rather roundabout and unexpected result of the triumph of the manipulatory science of mesmerism over fatalistic phrenology.

XVII

The Sage of Hyde Park

or

Success to the Shoemaker's Apprentice

WHEN MRS. EMMA WILLARD HAD
FINALLY PERSUADED THE STATE
OF NEW YORK TO GRANT HER
for her school a teacher of science for a few weeks each
year, her first choice for Professor of Chemistry had
been, for some reason she did not bother to explain,
Attorney J. Stanley Grimes. To make his lectures practical to the young ladies, he described to them the chem-
ical horrors produced in the female form by wine-
bibbing. One especially alert miss, recalling the Fowlers'
demonstrations, asked him to explain the relationship
between alcoholism and Alimentativeness.

The poser set Professor Grimes to studying Spurzheim more diligently than he had ever read Blackstone.
He emerged from his research convinced that the bumps
in the skull did indeed indicate the contents of the brain
but even surer that nobody had mapped out the right
locations. He drew up a diagram showing the position
of every faculty radically changed, the base passions

where the high virtues had hitherto been sought, and vice versa. Such topsy-turvy unorthodoxy was righteously opposed by the College of Phrenologists but got Professor Grimes enough customers to cause him to abandon the law for science. Those who had received derogatory readings at the Fowlers' Cabinet were assured of excellent ones from him.

As soon as he heard that the College had endorsed Pathetism, Professor Grimes hastened to Boston to demonstrate at the Tremont Temple his counter-science of Etherology. The strange alterations in character which Dr. Sunderland claimed to have produced by prodding Mary's skull had actually been effected according to the ex-attorney by the mysterious substance of Etherium—which had been actuated by the voice of her operator, but was comprehensible only to Professor Grimes—striking her ears. To make his theory convincing to the less cultured audiences before whom he demonstrated it after leaving Boston, he devised the technique later to become known as post-hypnotic suggestion.

His method was to invite to his hotel room twenty or more youths indigenous to the locality where he was to lecture, and magnetize them. While he had them entranced he would convey to them, through the medium of etherium, the information that they had become famous characters like Patrick Henry, George Washington or Spurzheim. When they awoke they would, of course, be unable to remember anything that had happened since Professor Grimes first took hold of their thumbs. The next night he would magnetize them in the Town Hall with magnificent effects.

Before his eyes had quite closed the youth who had been told that he was Patrick Henry would strike a dramatic pose and holler "Liberty or death." The one who had been called George Washington would hack at a small imaginary tree or start skimming silver dollars out over the auditorium. And he who had been designated Spurzheim would leap from the rostrum and rush among the audience, shouting "veneration," "ideality," and "marvelousness," as he bashed one customer after another over the head.

Their performances were so realistic that in the smaller towns of upstate New York the audiences, who knew nothing about modern science, were plain scared. They thought the ghosts of Washington, Henry and that foreigner whose name they didn't catch were actually animating these boys, who just a few hours before had been milking their cows, chopping their wood or chasing their daughters.

In Poughkeepsie among the local youths that Professor Grimes summoned to the Hatch Hotel was a seventeen-year-old shoemaker's apprentice from Hyde Park by the name of Andrew Jackson Davis. He was such poor magnetic material that he continued to stare open-mouthed and wide-awake at the etherologist's flaying arms and poking thumbs long after his companions, quicker to grasp what was expected of them, were all blinking, drowsing and drooping to the floor. Such blatant non-susceptibility disgusted Professor Grimes, who ordered the youth abruptly from the room.

Being dismissed for his stupidity was not a new experience for young Davis. The first shoemaker to whom he had been apprenticed had discharged him with the observation that the lout couldn't tell his last from a sole. But that night at the Town Hall when he saw his companions of the afternoon doing their stuff, and heard the neighbors say that they were actually feeling the spirits of the men they imitated, the mentally underprivileged youth for the first time in his life experienced the emotion of shame.

Not only was he named after a personage as famous as those whose life tags were being re-enacted, but the parents of Andrew Jackson Davis were noted throughout Dutchess County for their intimacy with the dead. His father generally needed a dozen or so noggins of rum under his belt in order to get really chummy with the shades with whom the Davises shared their shack, but his mother, drunk or sober, saw ghosts and talked with them familiarly whenever she felt like it.

The son and heir of this strangely talented couple was sent the next afternoon on an errand to the tailor shop. When its proprietor inquired what was eating him, the boy confessed his chagrin. Mr. Levinson was fortunately an educated man who possessed a copy of "A Letter to Dr. A. A. Bingham," which he already knew by heart. He told Andrew Jackson Davis that if he would only put himself in his hands he would soon have him doing fancier things than any of Professor Grimes' stooges. And he was.

Replacing his iron on the fire, Mr. Levinson began making passes at his visitor who within three minutes became deathly pale, frigidly cold, and said in a voice from which his adenoidal overtones were oddly missing, "I can see through the back of my head." When the tailor balanced a newspaper there the boy read it off column for column and word for word. This was more wonderful by far than anything Miss Brackett had done, for until that very minute Andrew Jackson Davis had never been able to read anything at all.

Tidings of his feat spread quickly through the township, and by nightfall more than a hundred Dutchess County residents had crowded into the tailor shop to witness the miracle. Andrew Jackson repeated the performance of the afternoon, interrupting the news broadcast at frequent intervals to inject gratuitous diagnoses of his auditors' ailments. The attendance at Professor Grimes' lectures fell off precipitously. Mr. Levinson left coats unsewed and breeches unpressed in order to develop to the limit the supernatural resources of the gifted goon.

Since, unlike the magnetizers of Providence, Boston and New York, the Poughkeepsie tailor was neither a licensed physician nor an ordained clergyman, he didn't quite dare to charge for the Davis diagnoses, but he had a better idea. He asked the entranced, shaking Andrew Jackson not only what ailed the neighbors but what would cure them. From a hastily assembled stock of herbs and groceries Levinson concocted the remedies as rapidly as the boy reeled them off—and sold them to the open-mouthed diagnosees.

After the pair had all of Dutchess County drinking their tonics and smearing their lotions, Levinson took his find on a curing tour. When they worked as far east as Bridgeport, they ran into trouble. Davis' simple prescriptions of mustard, pepper and penny-royal had satisfied the rural New Yorkers, but the citizens of the more urban sections of Connecticut demanded more complicated medication than a tramping tailor could devise.

The Reverend S. B. Brittain, a Universalist divine of Bridgeport, solved the problem to his own and Mr. Levinson's relief. Living with Preacher Brittain was his brother-in-law Dr. John Lyon, a learned but at the time insolvent "botanic physician," whom the minister persuaded to join up with the Poughkeepsie pair on a percentage basis. During their stay in Connecticut, then, Mr. Levinson acted only as the Davis magnetizer, while Dr. Lyon took over the role of apothecary.

It would have been a happy combination, except that Dr. Lyon brooded continually over his cut of the take. It was the smallest of the three, because he had come into the act last, yet he did the only real work. Presently he borrowed some magnetic literature, boned up on the sly, and one day, while Mr. Levinson was out

seeing the sights of New Haven, attempted to mesmerize Davis. Andrew Jackson had by now grown so agree-
ably impressible that he responded as readily to Dr.
Lyon's passes as to anyone else's. It was while the
apothecary had him entranced that he began his lifelong habit of referring to himself in the third person as
the Sage and the Prophet. It was also under Dr. Lyon's
tutelage that he acquired the trick of leaving his body
sitting comfortably in a chair while his soul soared into
the spirit world and picked up pertinent bits of
information.

The Davis soul returned from one such excursion
with the announcement that the Prophet would soon
have a revelation, which when written down and published would "put the Bible in the shade" and certainly
net $50,000—but only on one condition: that the Sage
discharge Mr. Levinson and promote Dr. Lyon to magnetizer and manager. So Mr. Levinson went back to his
pants pressing—and Dr. Lyon got the surprise of his
life.

Out of reach of the magnetic influence of the tailor,
the speech of Andrew Jackson Davis reverted to its
Hyde Park vernacular. The new thoughts that his soul
brought back from the Beyond were always lofty and
inspiring, but the mortal mouth expressed them in
double negatives and grammatical oddities that compared ill with the purity of the Book that he was going
to knock cold. It was impossible to transmit his words
to paper, and Andrew Jackson himself could not write.

The spirits were again consulted and suggested that the Prophet engage as his Scribe William Fishbough, another Universalist minister wise in the lore of Swedenborg but temporarily without a pulpit. The new combination worked splendidly. Even under the best of conditions the Sage's diction was a little difficult to understand; the tremors that shook him when entranced made his speech unintelligible to all save those who knew him intimately. But now, to make sure that not one syllable he uttered should be lost to posterity, Dr. Lyon repeated each word the Prophet spoke just as it began to roll off his tongue, and the Scribe wrote it down grammatically. The result, if still not completely intelligible, was rather elegant prose.

The three partners divided their working hours nicely too. The mornings were spent in medicine-making; the afternoons and evenings, with the Prophet rigid upon the floor and until he went to sleep for true, in collaborating on the "Divine Revelations."

From Connecticut Dr. Lyon took the Sage of Hyde Park to Providence, where Miss Brackett and President Wayland gazed enviously upon him; then to the Orange Mountain Water Cure where, while the Davis soul kept up its celestial soarings, the Davis backsides got some needed refreshment in a flowing sitz bath; and finally on to New York City where the three engaged rooms at 24 Vesey Street from Mrs. Gors, the boardinghouse keeper upon whom Dr. Shew had introduced the bath with affusion.

The New York stop was at first a spiritual disappointment and a financial flop; for the City of the Whirlpool was already so crammed with magnetic healers that it just couldn't tolerate another—even though he traveled with a botanic apothecary as proficient as Dr. Lyon. When the spirits were consulted, they suggested that a few of the most prominent and best educated New Yorkers be invited to Vesey Street to witness the Divine Dictation. Even that presented a difficulty.

The first section of the first volume of the Revelation was almost completed and that was difficult enough to understand even by those who had repeated and transcribed every word of it. Anyone breaking in on the performance at this late date might mistake the whole thing for double talk. William Fishbough, again on the advice of the spirits, sought out his old friend and fellow Universalist, Horace Greeley, and explained the predicament to him. Greeley obligingly published in the next day's *Tribune*, under the heading "Remarkable Phenomena," a synopsis of the First Book of the Revelation that was considered clear enough to enable a select audience to follow the Second, and advised the Scribe about the celebrities to be invited to the pre-view.

Since the Divine Revelation had theological and literary as well as scientific implications, the audience that appeared at Vesey Street the next afternoon was more varied and far more distinguished than the group of specialists that had witnessed Mary's performance. At the head of the theologians was the Reverend Joel

Parker who had been imported from Boston in 1830, because there was not at that time in all New York a minister liberal enough to lead the Free Church movement initiated by the Finney revivals. He had subsequently displayed such talent for handling magdalene societies and female asylums that he had been promoted to the presidency of the Union Theological Seminary. Corralling the men of letters was Nathaniel P. Willis, the darling of society, not only in New York but in every American city and European capital to which he had taken his handsome figure and observant mind.

This son of the founder of the *Youth's Companion*, the first magazine written exclusively for children, had just the proper preparation for becoming "the topmost bubble on the wave of Fashion." From the Latin School in Boston, where he remembered Ralph Waldo Emerson as a social inferior, to Phillips Andover and to Yale he progressed with increasing honors and popularity. His literary taste was so marked that the year after his graduation he was selected as editor of *The Token*, the most important gift book of 1828. Moving to New York, he displayed such a genius for making social doings seem as lively in print as they always were when he attended them in person, that Parke Benjamin made him European correspondent of the *New World*. So that his readers could get the ultimate in pleasure from his columns, Willis advised them always to think of him writing at a rosewood desk upon which an ever-fresh japonica shed its perfume, while a French valet hovered near to refresh him at his labors with vintage wine and olives. The idea had taken on so well that Japonicadom had become the inevitable synonym for Fashion.

One might have thought that the meeting for the first time in Mrs. Gors' front parlor of two men whose spheres of influence were as severely opposed as those of Joel Parker and Nathaniel Willis would have caused such magnetic disturbances that the Sage's somnambulant dictation would have been rendered impossible. But Horace Greeley had warded off that calamity in the person he had suggested—since editorial duties and unfamiliarity with the best social usage prevented him from assuming the office himself—as entrepreneur to the Prophet. The person so favored was Rufus Griswold, the liberal thinker par excellence, an unsuccessful preacher turned literary critic.

Having firmly established himself as the best paid writer of the times, Griswold could afford the luxury of bringing lesser scriveners to public attention. As leading promoter of pure Americanism in art, he had already put over the four most talented minor poets among the authoresses, Mrs. Osgood, Mrs. Oakes Smith, and the incomparable Cary girls, Phoebe and Alice—the dowdy sisters at whom Mrs. Osgood was cracking when she referred to literary ladies with dirty gloves and holes in their stockings. Griswold was now ready for a flier into international, or rather interplanetary, philosophy. His soothing presence laid the diverse influences shooting out from Messrs. Willis and Parker as he introduced the star performer to his audience.

The Sage, the dope, as familiar as he was with the universe of the spirits, was so ignorant of the world of men that he didn't know one of these distinguished gentlemen from the other. But having been warned that important preachers would be present he sought out the most other-worldly looking person there and recited to him the little speech that had been impressed upon him, "Your ideas about ultimates, sir, are strictly and philosophically true."

To which Edgar Allan Poe, the person so addressed, replied, "There surely *cannot* be more things in Heaven and earth than are dreamt of, oh, Andrew Jackson Davis, in your Philosophy."

The tom-noddy was so pleased to have someone speak directly to him again—since Mr. Levinson had left, he had been addressed always obliquely as the Sage or the Prophet or just plain Him—that there was some trouble in getting him stalled and bedded down for the séance. The gentleman who knew such fine phrases and dispersed them so graciously must, he felt, be impressed by a shade even more sublime than Swedenborg. He was pleased when he peeked through his blinking eyes during the dictation to see that his new friend was taking notes almost as industriously as the Reverend Mr. Fishbough.

Rufus Griswold was not so pleased. He knew Poe better than anyone else in New York did; he had in fact succeeded him as editor of *Graham's* back in Philadelphia, and he had good reason to suspect the good faith behind his attendance at this solemn occasion.

Griswold, as much as he loved his role of celebrity-maker, had hesitated to introduce Poe to his transcendental friends in New York, for the Virginian had attended the dissolute university of his native state and had, while there, Griswold knew for a fact, absorbed the notoriously pantheistic ideas of that institution's founder. Griswold had therefore been very put out with Willis—who was usually so critical of other people, even saying that Fanny Kemble's declared passion for horses was just a newcastle-ing of cheese-cake when she dismounted at Delmonico's in her masculine habit—when Willis had confessed after working with Poe for a few months on the *Mirror* that he felt almost a reverence for the man. And now to have the Sage of Hyde Park simpering like a rustic maiden just because Poe threw a misquotation from Shakespeare at him was entirely out of order. Griswold's intuition warned him that the man who had recently startled New York with his Balloon Hoax might have come to Mrs. Gors' to gather material for another and much more serious imposture.

But when the results of Poe's note-taking that afternoon were finally published as the "Mesmeric Revelation" and "The Case of M. Valdemar"—both of them discourses carried on by a magnetized subject beyond his death and in the latter tale beyond his physical dissolution—Griswold regretted his suspicions. Poe's sympathetic treatment of his subject persuaded him that Poe had at last renounced the atheism of Thomas Jefferson. From all over New England and from Germany Poe received letters from sincere believers praising the absolute veracity of his "Mesmeric Revelation." As a result—so wrote Rufus Griswold, the ex-Baptist preacher who had been born to illiterate parents on a New England farm—the man from Richmond was received for the first time "into circles capable both of the appreciation and the production of literature."

The next year Poe gleefully stated in *Godey's* that both of his transcendentalist pieces had been written in the same spirit that prompted the Balloon Hoax. His nose thumbing was reprinted in the first collected edition of his works, in the preface to which Griswold still insisted that "The Case of M. Valdemar" and the "Mesmeric Revelation" were Edgar Allan Poe's finest works.

This curious fact has been dimmed by the more shocking fact that in that same preface Griswold spread the tale that the man whose work he was appraising for posterity was among many other anti-social things a rapist. But Rufus Griswold was not only Poe's literary executor, he was in his own opinion and that of many others the literary arbiter of his day. As such he was willing that Poe's reputation as a brilliant writer of short stories and fugitive poems should survive his death, but he had—in the interest of mesmerism, Swedenborgianism, Fourierism and all the other doctrines that constituted the literary credo of the liberals of that day—to inter Poe the critic along with his liquor-soaked bones. For Poe alone among the literary men of the middle nineteenth century had the intelligence and the education to recognize that all those isms stemmed from the same source. He knew that they were not wonderously new and hopeful, but as old and evil as irrationality itself. All his criticism was informed by an impassioned intolerance of these strange doctrines and the barrier to thought which was their common bond.

Poe could not know that within less than a hundred years of his death a mystic belief in irrational panaceas would begin to corrode the body politic and the whole structure of our life, but he saw clearly during his lifetime that it was ruining American literature. He laughed at Greeley and Brisbane for their credulity, but when he saw men of talent displaying the same "insanity," he tried to warn them where they were heading. It was painful to him that a star-filled old gas-bag like Bronson Alcott should be the dictator of New England thinking. Poe said, in effect, that if Emerson would stop his hero-worship of the Prussian who wrote under the name of Thomas Carlyle, he would come to his American senses; that if Nathaniel Hawthorne and that mountain would only quit making Fourieristic faces at one another, Hawthorne could fulfill his great promise.

But the transcendentalists did not want to listen to

Poe, and Griswold felt it his duty to erase his criticisms of them. He could neither destroy nor tamper with Poe's actual words, for they had already been published and widely read; so to destroy their value Griswold adopted a method that is as old as the irrationality which Poe was fighting and which is growing increasingly familiar today. He set out to prove that Poe's criticisms could not be valid because they were written by a man devoid of "moral susceptibility" and impelled only by a "cold, repellent cynicism" and a "hatred of his fellowmen."

How well Griswold succeeded in demolishing Poe as a bulwark against the wave of unreason can be determined by the feeble attempts of those who have tried to clear his name. All of his contemporaries—and most of his subsequent biographers—have been, to use his own words as applied to Mary Gove, too "tinctured by the mysticism of the transcendentalists" to comprehend what the shooting was all about. Certainly John Neal, who was eventually shocked to sympathy with him by his death, could not. Willis and Mrs. Osgood, who cared more than anything about the gracious manners at which they along with Poe excelled, were intent only upon refuting the libel that the Virginian was a boor.

As for the charge that Poe did not love his wife, Mrs. Gove's reply seems directed—with her boasted clairvoyance—not so much to Griswold as to a future liberal editor who was to write that Poe was incapable of doing anything of the sort. Mary Gove, always eager to overload anyone she admired with her own virtues, wrote that Poe not only truly loved Virginia but "that he loved other beautiful and loveful spirits also."

As to his religion Poe could have agreed with his contemporary Disraeli who said that all sensible men have the same religion but being sensible they keep quiet about it. Sex and religion were inextricably bound together by all of Poe's planning contemporaries and because he kept his mouth shut on the one two-barreled topic, he was accused of aberrations in both fields.

XVIII

The Spirits Court the Fox Sisters

MOST OF THE AUDIENCE ATTENDING THE SAGE'S FIRST DICTATION IN NEW YORK WERE LESS PUZZLED about Mr. Poe than by the star performer himself, for there was about the Prophet's utterances a vague familiarity, as of a half-forgotten dream. As the afternoon wore on this reminiscent quality became more recognizable.

The Sage's certainty that mortal life was an illusion; his declaration that God's body was infinite wisdom, His mind infinite love; his description of the Spirit Worlds—of Hell where unregenerate souls went of their own free wills; and of Heaven where all three glorious orders of angels, natural, spiritual and celestial, lived and looked and loved, for all their glory and divinity, much like the illusory mortals on this nonexistent planet; his persistent reiteration of the number "three" and of the words "sphere," "plane," "correspondence" and "affinity"—why, all of it, so his guests finally realized, sounded like an echo of the more obtuse articles in *The Harbinger* and the conversations at Henry James' dinner parties.

The entranced Andrew Jackson Davis was apparently paraphrasing Swedenborg; or perhaps quoting him word for word. No one at this first audition could be quite sure, for though the philosophy of the New Jerusalem was clear and simple to the transcendentalists of New England, few among the most prominent and highly educated New Yorkers—except of course Mrs. Mowatt when she too was somnambulant—could make heads or tails of it.

This important point was cleared up the next afternoon by the most learned member of President Parker's faculty, George Bush, the only professor of theology in the whole world who was as familiar with the writings of Swedenborg and Mesmer as with those of Mohammed and God.

When this spit-and-image of Nicholas Biddle heard Andrew Jackson Davis proclaim the second installment of the second section of his Divine Revelation, he said that the utterances of the Sage of Hyde Park were indeed almost identical with some of the simpler passages of *Arcana Coelestia,* but that only proved how especially well favored was the Prophet's view of the celestial spheres. It was quite evident to Professor Bush that the divine soul of Swedenborg was using Andrew Jackson Davis as his "medium," repeating through the mesmerized Davis mouth the very same sentiments that the mortal Swedenborg hand had written while confined to this illusory earth. Andrew Jackson, temporarily aroused from his magnetic stupor and appraised of this supposition, allowed that it might be so.

To some it might seem irreverent to imagine that the angelic soul of Swedenborg, which was as learned in the highest Heaven as its corresponding body had been on the lowliest earth plane, should choose as its first medium of inter-spherical communication an illiterate, uncouth shoemaker's apprentice—but not to one who knew the history of Swedenborg's eighty-six-year so-journ on this planet as thoroughly as Professor Bush.

God Himself had appeared to Swedenborg in sur-roundings not dissimilar to a Dutchess County cemetery, allowed him to gaze upon His Heavens and introduced him to His angels. That was why at the age of fifty-nine Swedenborg had resigned his position as Assessor to the Swedish Board of Mines to devote the rest of his life to perfecting himself in the Hebrew language—so that he could converse with his new friend in His native tongue. Not even the most devout New Church mem-ber, Professor Bush pointed out, could deny that the erudition of the Lord God Jehovah *might* be as superior to that of Emanuel Swedenborg as Swedenborg's was to Andrew Jackson Davis'.

There was one point upon which Professor Bush felt constrained to caution the Seer. That was his habit of frequenting graveyards and striking up an acquaintance with any ghost that accosted him. It was a trait that he had probably acquired from his mother, but if indulged in indiscriminately could become dangerous. His chance conversations with false spirits—and there were as many such, he must remember, now living in the celestial spheres as there had ever been evil persons residing on this earth—probably accounted for the minor deviations of the Divine Revelation from the *Arcana Coelestia*. These were not so many or so important that Professor Bush could not correct them in a few easy lessons. But until the whole matter of spiritual affinities was fully revealed to him, the impressible young medium should shun all intercourse with ghosts of whose identity he was uncertain, especially those he suspected of being females. Should he after only twenty years of mortal existence acquire for his affinity throughout the ages the soul of an unscrupulous woman, she could—by misinforming him about Heaven and Hell, and confounding in his mind good with evil—injure his mortal soul much worse than any harlot from the Five Points could harm his ungainly body.

After Professor Bush had endorsed his vision, the Sage received another suggestion from the true spirits. Since the dictating of the Revelation was monopolizing the Davis cerebral power at such a rate as to leave it no strength for healing, and consequently no pecuniary income, the spirits thought it would be a good idea to make the dictation henceforth in some public place— say Clinton Hall, if agreeable to the Fowlers—and to charge a reasonable fee for those who witnessed the miracle. As a consequence, during the next eighteen months the Sage, assisted by his Operator and his Scribe,

gave exactly one hundred and fifty-seven public readings in New York. His audiences were every bit as
distinguished and learned, and fortunately a great deal
larger, than that which attended the original party in
Vesey Street.

Not even when the Prophet, somewhat confused
about Professor Bush's assurance that a mortal woman
was less hurtful than a spherical spirit, chose as his first
affinity not a celestial soul but Mrs. Lapham, a comely
and notorious divorcée, was there any slackening of attendance. If anything, his audience became more distinguished, for by then, the Sage himself having been taken
up by the Fourierists, his spiritual utterances had taken
on deep overtones of social significance, and of course
messing around with a divorcée is no great deterrent to
a career devoted to social uplift.

It was well that the Prophet had gone in for broad
social planning, for his claim to being the only citizen
of this world able to commune at will with the denizens
of the Other was soon challenged by two pretty little
girls who lived even farther upstate than Dutchess
County.

In December 1847, Mr. and Mrs. Fox of Rochester
moved with their large family to the village of Hydesville in Wayne County. Mr. Fox was mildly surprised
to find his rent so much lower than his neighbors'; the
neighbors were not reticent about explaining why. No
Wayne County native would live in the house for the

same reason that its last tenant, Michael Weekman, had quit it in haste. It was haunted.

Often Mr. Weekman, reading his paper by candle-light after the rest of his family had gone to bed, would hear distinct raps on the roof; yet no matter how quickly he opened the door or how carefully he searched the porch and the yard, he found no human being lurking about his premises. The explanation of the rappings was obvious, especially after eight-year-old Susan Weekman formed the habit of waking up in the middle of the night and screaming for her mamma. Each time, so the terrified child sobbed, a cold hand had passed over the bed-clothes and rested on her face. The visitations were particularly frequent on windy nights, when her father, waiting in the dark to catch the rapper, declared he was almost pulled off his feet when he suddenly jerked open the door.

Ordinarily the Foxes would have got out of such a house as quickly as the Weekmans, especially Mrs. Fox, who was nervous and mortally afraid of haunts. But recently the entire family had been converted to Methodism. The pastor back in Rochester, thinking to keep them interested in the pioneers of the sect, had lent Mr. Fox the *Memoirs of the Wesley Family*, a narrative manufactured from the writings of John Wesley. Mr. Fox found most of it pretty tedious, but one short passage he liked well enough to read aloud. In this John told how when he was a boy of thirteen his whole family had been kept awake at night, and, he wasn't ashamed to admit, badly frightened by eerie rappings in their Epworth home. It seemed to the Foxes a good omen to be living in a house so uncannily like the birthplace of Methodism's founder.

Yet for three months, strain their ears as they might, the Foxes heard none but natural and human sounds in Hydesville. Then on the night of March 20, 1848, manifestations even more thrilling than they had hoped for began to occur.

Mamma and Papa were just settling in their goosefeathers, and across the room their two youngest daughters, Margaretta who was "about fourteen" and Catherine "about twelve" (Mrs. Fox seldom remembered the number, much less the exact ages of her offspring), were presumably dead in sleep, when the clatter began, not on the roof but right there in the bedroom. There was certainly Something there, knocking on the floor and moving the furniture around. The girls whispered that their bed was heaving so they had to hold to the headboard to keep from falling off. The father's shaking fingers at last got a candle lit, and as was to be expected there was no human in the room other than the Foxes. The furniture was where it belonged, but the rapping had not stopped.

Both adults were speechless, but Catherine, showing remarkable courage for one so young, snapped her fingers. The Sound snapped his right back at her. Margaretta commanded, "Now do as I do. Count one, two, three, four." She then clapped her hands four times and the Sound made the same number of knocks. Mamma, her curiosity overcoming her terror, whispered, "Count up to ten," and the Thing did so. Urged on by the girls it tapped out the ages of all her children more accurately than she could have done herself.

Mrs. Fox now pulled herself together sufficiently to ask, "Are you human?" The silence in the bedroom grew unbearable until it was broken by the tremulous but inevitable question, "Are you a spirit?" There came a resounding whack, after which the spirit obligingly knocked out the information that it was the father of two mortal sons and three living daughters, and had itself been dead two years. To Mrs. Fox's last three queries, "Are you an injured spirit?" "Did someone in this house injure you?" and "Are you buried under this house?" it gave loud, enthusiastic assent.

Though the knocks kept up till daylight the elder Foxes were much too disturbed by the information they had already received to find courage to ask for more. It was bad enough to think they were living over a private burying ground, but what to do about the knowledge that a murderer had lived there before them? Should they keep it secret or risk telling the neighbors about Mr. Weekman? When the rapping started up again the next night they decided they must tell—otherwise the Spirit might wreak on them the vengeance intended for the Weekmans.

The Sound had no more trouble convincing the open-minded neighbors than the Foxes. The strongest men started digging in the cellar, while the bravest formed a posse in search of Mr. Weekman. A Mr. Ellis, a little more cautious than the others, sat right down on the girls' bed, where the knocks were always the loudest, and asked the Sound point blank if Mr. Weekman was its murderer. There was no response, and Mr. Ellis said sharply, "Well, then, who did kill you?"

The bedstead shook violently as Margaretta and Catherine clutched each other, buried their heads under the covers and let out smothered gasps which on a less solemn occasion might have sounded like giggles. The Spirit began to rap hysterically, knocking several times, stopping, and starting in again. Mr. Ellis counted three taps and then, after a pause, eighteen—which was clearly not a very intelligible answer to his question. Maybe, someone suggested—in the excitement nobody remembered just who—the Spirit was no longer counting but trying to spell by rapping out the alphabet. If this were so, then the murderer's initials were C. R., which were definitely not those of the hunted Michael Weekman.

Mr. Ellis then urged the Sound to spell out some more answers. It was a little slow about catching on to this—or perhaps just a poor speller—and stubbornly refused to reveal its own name. Yet before the second night was done the company was satisfied that the Spirit had been an itinerant peddler who had been foully done to death for the $500 he unluckily carried about with him. The good people of Wayne were proud of the distinction that had come to their county.

As soon as Mrs. Fox caught up on her sleep, she wrote of the wonderous happenings to her elder daughter, Mrs. Leah Fish, a widow in her early thirties and still living in Rochester. Leah replied by the next post, asking that Margaretta be allowed to come to live with her. Things now became more mysterious than ever.

Though the knockings continued in Hydesville, they also started up in Rochester. And the ghost—or the part of a ghost—that followed Margaretta to the city proved to be more adept at spelling than the presence that remained in the country with Catherine. Whenever Mrs. Fish was in the same room with her sister, it could spell with fair accuracy choice bits of Rochester gossip. But Leah Fish, less impulsive than her parents, did not invite all her neighbors to chat with the Spirit. She guarded Margaretta and the recently arrived Catherine jealously while the Sound was dissociating itself from the murdered peddler and making connections with spirits of more interest to the citizens of Rochester.

It was to get the latest news of their own departed friends and relatives that they crowded into the Corinthian Hall when Mrs. Fish finally exhibited the sisters to the public. Everyone agreed that the experience was well worth the dollar charged for admission. Even the inevitable Committee of the city's leading skeptics, who had confidently expected to declare the whole proceedings fraudulent, were convinced by the cheery tappings of their dear ones. Yet for all that, Catherine and Margaretta Fox might have remained local upstate oddities had not Supreme Court Justice John Worth Edmonds, who was visiting his friend Chancellor Whittesey at the time, been taken to Corinthian Hall by his host.

Judge Edmonds was by far the favorite jurist of the nineteenth century liberals, a man who never allowed his sworn duty to uphold so-called law and order to stand in the way of his higher duty to the higher laws toward which his intuition impelled him. Nor had he allowed his social position to keep him from becoming an enthusiastic member of numerous temperance, anti-slavery and non-interventionist societies—associations not favored by the upper crust at the time he joined them. His favorite organization was one that he had originated and which was composed beside himself entirely of students and graduates of Sing Sing, in whose behalf he had striven mightily since at the beginning of his political career he had been appointed prison inspector. Though few of the laws liberalizing penal procedure which he advocated took effect during his life, his political enemies agreed with his friends that they were "very advanced."

Judge Edmonds was also a staunch alumnus of Union College and a warm friend of President Nott and those two other illustrious sons of Union, Francis Wayland and Thomas Brownell. Through them he kept in as close touch with science as with the penal institutions of New York State. He was therefore able to detect in the Fox girls' performance a quality which the less learned citizens of Rochester missed—its similarity to the trance readings of Andrew Jackson Davis. Though Margaretta and Catherine lacked the cultural background to recognize it, they were undoubtedly in touch with the celestial spheres described in the Divine Revelation. They, too, were spiritual mediums.

Judge Edmonds also noted a superiority in the sisters' communications, as noisy and monosyllabic as they were, over the Prophet's. While the Sage of Hyde Park communed only with the soul of Swedenborg, and always in almost unintelligible language, Margaretta and Catherine seemed able to make direct contact with nearly everyone in Heaven—and in Hell too, no doubt, had they wished to do so—and get messages so simple that even they could understand them.

Judge Edmond's enthusiasm for the girls inspired him to found another organization, The First Spiritualists of America, in their honor, and to neglect his work with the convicts to promote it. The intellectuals who had attended the Davis readings were naturally eager to join, but the Judge was also able to interest the few practical scientists in the country, who had hitherto stood out against the modern philosophies, in spiritualism. Notable among these were James Mapes, President of the Mechanics Institute and "Father of Scientific Agriculture"; Robert Hare, Professor of Chemistry at the University of Pennsylvania and lifelong research associate of Yale's Professor Silliman; and Horace Day,

who took time off from the fight he was having with
Charles Goodyear over who had first invented vul-
canized rubber to join with his scientific colleagues in
attesting the authenticity of the rappings.

Soon running up to Rochester to spend the week-end
in spiritual rapport with Catherine and Margaretta became a custom among Judge Edmonds' friends. Finally
Phineas T. Barnum, who was at the time doing his best
to crash Society, also made the trip—and a deal with
Leah Fish to exhibit the girls in his museum in the room
that had recently been vacated by his famous petrified
mermaid. The crowds that paid two dollars a head to
hear the Sound tap out its messages were far more distinguished than those which for cheaper fees had gaped
at Chang and Eng and Joyce Heath, the one hundred
and ninety-nine-year-old nurse of George Washington
—his old black mummy, the wags called her.

The psychical excitement brought on by this exhibition caused the Sound to split its personality again, into
as many pieces as an exploding atom; and each frag-
ment attached itself to some visitor to the museum and
accompanied him home, there to begin its own thump-
ings and bumpings. Soon throughout the entire nation,
from Maine to the westernmost reaches of Wisconsin,
in the houses of travelers recently returned from New
York the joists were jumping from the game of Puss-in-
the-corner being played incessantly by the spirited
furniture.

XIX

The Spirits Come to the Aid
of Truth

THE VISIT OF MRS. FISH AND THE MISSES FOX TO NEW YORK CITY WAS THE OCCASION OF MUCH BRILLIANT entertaining. When Rufus Griswold was their host his guests included William Cullen Bryant, George Bancroft, Fenimore Cooper, Nathaniel Willis, George Ripley, General Lyman, Dr. Frances, and the Reverend Joseph Tuckerman, who had preached the most distinguished sermon over Spurzheim and made the trip to New York especially to attend these happier festivities. As the evening wore on, so Willis reported, the guests of honor won the unstinted respect of all present.

The same distinguished company was joined the next evening at the Horace Greeleys' soirée by Miss Jenny Lind who was also appearing in New York under the Barnum aegis but at Tripler's Hall rather than in the Museum. Among the fabulous Jenny's many distinctions there was one that has been seldom mentioned. She was the first person to notice that Margaretta Fox always moved her nether limbs whenever the spirits spoke. When Miss Lind called attention to this fact, the Greeleys' other guests attributed it to professional jealousy—several whispered that Willis, who had been extolling her charms for years, had oversold them on the Nightingale's modesty and amiability.

Mere cattiness was scarcely the motive which prompted a group of physicians to make the same observation in Buffalo less than six weeks later. Mrs. Fish was teaming with Margaretta in that city because the Greeleys had insisted that Catherine prolong her visit to them. Even with her lack of schooling, Mrs. Greeley felt that she would make a more amiable house guest than the late lamented Margaret Fuller.

Mrs. Fish was properly indignant when she read in the *Courier and Enquirer* a communication signed by three professors of medicine at the University of Buffalo saying it was their considered opinion that Margaretta Fox's knee and ankle bones accounted for the famed Rochester Rappings. Leah Fish immediately inserted a Card in the paper inviting the skeptical gentlemen to her rooms to make any experiments they wished upon herself and her sister. The gentlemen accepted and were more realistic in their examination than the challenger could have suspected. They held the girls' legs for an hour in a soundless room. Only when their tired fingers relaxed could they hear mild rappings and feel distinct movements in the knees. Before the detailed report of their findings appeared in the medical journals, Dr. Charles Lee, one of the professors, sent a less technical version of them to Horace Greeley. In it he said that anyone who possessed the not uncommon knack of snapping the knee joints, and also knew the ventriloquists' trick of diverting an audience's attention *away* from the source of a sound, could duplicate the phenomena that sounded the Fox family to fame.

Horace Greeley printed Dr. Lee's letter in the *Tribune* with the non-committal comment that if the noises actually occurred as the physician said they did, then his theory concerning their origin seemed adequate. This same ambiguous attitude was adopted by most of the other members of the Society of Spiritualists. Judge Edmonds and his more sophisticated colleagues in New York were not reluctant to pass up Margaretta and Catherine Fox.

The rappings, so exciting at first, had with repetition grown monotonous and irritating. It was a little humiliating for college-educated men like judges, editors, professors and bishops to have to take two silly country girls into their confidence whenever they wished to communicate with their equals in the spirit world. Especially since Margaretta's and Catherine's vocabularies were so limited that they even had William Shakespeare and Francis Bacon, when they argued over which of them had written England's greatest dramas, talking like Wayne county hill-billies. Nor were the incessant knockings conducive to the highest intellectual thought. Professor Hare consulted another eminent physicist, and the founder of the school in Philadelphia where he now taught that science, about the auditory interference.

The Spirits Come to the Aid of Truth

Benjamin Franklin upon the celestial spheres must have repented the experiments in his backyard in Passy, for he impressed upon Professor Hare the directions for constructing the Spiritoscope—an elaborate piece of apparatus, equipped with letters and moving gadgets, by means of which Franklin and his fellow shades could spell out their messages without making any noise at all. Most mediums throughout the country soon simplified this device into the habit of clutching slate and pencil just before they fell into a trance and allowing the spirits to guide their fingers as they wrote out the messages. Others fell back on the Davis technique of speaking their lines while somnambulant and having a scribe write them down. Baptist and Methodist ministers who developed especially strong clairvoyant powers preferred young and pretty girls as their scribes.

As speaking and writing supplanted knocking as the standard mode of inter-spherical communication, the tone and the number of the messages increased. Soon there were more than six hundred professional mediums and more than a million professed spiritualists who, though amateurs, got excellent results at the weekly or daily séances they held in one another's homes. Families who went in seriously for communing with their dead had special séance rooms built on to their houses.

The most profitable of the séance rooms was probably that maintained by the Reverend Adin Ballou for the benefit of the fifty-six persons who had joined with him in founding a colony of Christian Communists at

Hopedale, Massachusetts. He had been training his eighteen-year-old son Augustus to become his successor as ruler of the flock when the youth was transmitted Above. Each day thereafter Augustus would return to the Hopedale séance room and through the voice of his sister Abbie give his father advice on scientific agriculture and equitable real estate values. So efficient was this arrangement that within a few years both the acreage and the membership of the Colony doubled and the worth of the property increased from four to forty thousand dollars.

But of all the spiritual gatherings that which was known as the Sacred Circle and met bi-weekly at the home of Judge Edmonds was the most renowned. There Brisbane, Greeley, Willis, Griswold, Henry Ward Beecher, William Fishbough and Bishop Jonathan Wainwright came regularly—and Emerson, Garrison, Theodore Parker and Charles Sumner, when they were in town—to talk with William Penn, Mrs. Hemans, Napoleon, St. Peter and Voltaire, who was admitted when he gave convincing proof that in Heaven he had finally got religion.

The Circle was considerably enlarged during its first twelve months, for during that time Fenimore Cooper and Henry Clay died and Major Raines of the Army was killed in an accident. All three appeared in the Edmonds' drawing-room at approximately the same time they did in less usual surroundings, and were able to give the Circlers a round by round description of their

reception on the various spheres. Not infrequently the
meetings were attended by spirits whom the more mundane members did not recognize, for though earthly
admittance was restricted, no earnest soul was ever
turned away, for often the anonymous shades transmitted the most important messages.

A touching instance of this was the unexpected appearance in the Circle of the Captain of the *S.S. Arctic*
recently sunk off Newfoundland, whose name the members did not learn until some weeks later when the
casualty list was made public. Accompanied by his crew,
the Captain explained to Judge Edmonds that in mortal
life he had been a pretty rough customer and hadn't
given as much thought as he should have to spiritual
matters. So would the Judge, please, tell him just the
proper procedure in passing through the Pearly Gates.
Judge Edmonds graciously complied.

Though this was a particularly urgent case, none of
the spirits who met with the Judge's group of distinguished mortals were allowed to waste their time in idle
chatter. There was work for them to do. Because they
could flit about the earth as instantaneously as through
more ethereal spheres and could cross thresholds barred
to living men, they were made special investigators of
the state of the nation. Mary Magdalene, for instance,
investigated events related to the Women's Rights
movement. Other shades, according to their former
specialties, reported on other phases of the national life
of particular interest to liberals: vagrancy, mendicancy,

public baths, education, intemperance, lodging houses, jails, ventilation and perfidious public figures who needed to be kicked out of office.

The reports were so complete and appalling that Judge Edmonds started a magazine, also called *The Sacred Circle*, so that the public could read them and write their Congressmen to do something about the conditions. The first number of *The Sacred Circle* carried this announcement:

"It will be the purpose of this work to advance Truth in every form and shape: to discuss Radical Moral Reform, Radical Intellectual Reform—the Reform of the times—in political, mercantile and mechanical relations; to advocate Liberty, positively and unhesitatingly, in the full and in the abstract; to examine the condition of our Country in every part, as a whole, and in the several States, Counties and Towns; to elevate the existing relations of Society; to form new relations, based on the principles of Spiritual Philosophy; and to develop those means which shall harmonize every element and instrumentality of Society one with another."

Judge Edmonds' editorial duties kept him conferring so constantly with the spirits that there was always a band of illustrious shades accompanying him wherever he went. He got into the habit of asking Washington, Penn, Swedenborg and Bacon to sit with him at the sessions of the Supreme Court. Whenever an especially knotty problem arose he would ask their opinion and insist that his fellow justices abide by it. His colleagues grumbled a little at this innovation, but it so greatly enhanced John Worth Edmonds' reputation among the liberals and intellectuals that he was elected first President of the Union League Club.

Aside from the jealous jurists, there was another group of men who did not understand how well accompanied Judge Edmonds was at all hours of the day and night. These were the husbands of the pretty young mediums who often found it necessary to consult him on higher matters at odd hours. During the summer when his wife and daughters were away at Saratoga, the Judge always had Mrs. Hemans or the Virgin Mary or some other respectable matron present as chaperon during these interviews in his seemingly deserted house. Though the materialistic husbands tried to insinuate that the chaperons were somewhat remiss in their duties, Judge Edmonds' reputation as a family man and his standing in the best social circles kept them from doing more than whisper their vague suspicions.

When, however, Dr. George T. Dexter, co-editor of *The Sacred Circle*, was forced to leave New York because of a crime which even the frank newspapers of that day forbore to mention, that was another matter. John F. Whitney, who had tried with *The Pathfinder* to start a rival to the Circle and had failed miserably, decided he could at least cash in on what he knew about his fellow spiritualists. After diligently checking the private lives of all the professional mediums in the

Northern States, Mr. Whitney made public the following facts:

"Of the 300 public mediums who have been married nearly a half have absolved their conjugal relations. A large proportion of the remainder have abandoned the bed of their partners; many are cohabiting with affinities by mutual consent of husband and wife; a still greater number are living in promiscuous concubinage." And, in case anyone should doubt his figures, Mr. Whitney gave the names of the more prominent mediums who had "gone the road to destruction," leaving broken hearts, illegitimate children and waves of suicides in their wake. The incidence of adultery among former Baptist and Methodist ministers was appalling.

The publication of Mr. Whitney's report caused a "volcano" in New York City, where most of the mediums had their headquarters, that shook the whole nation. The public recalled that spirit rapping had been born in the same section of New York State that had spawned Mormonism twenty years before, and that there was a curious similarity between the circumstances surrounding the Revelation of Andrew Jackson Davis and the vision of that earlier Seer, Prophet and Revelator, Joseph Smith.

The First President of the Latter Day Saints had found his message to humanity in a golden volume on a hill near Palmyra, New York. The lettering on the stones was so strange that Joseph Smith, who like so many other leaders was illiterate, could not read them until he put on the pair of spectacles that were conveniently secreted with the manuscript. But when he adjusted the two lenses—Urim for Light and Thummim for Perfection—he found in the golden book the ordinance that a man to become a saint must take more than one wife. Andrew Jackson Davis, of course, had got his Revelation more elegantly by going in spirit straight to Heaven and learning it from Swedenborg. He brought back no eyeglasses with him, so only the Sage, his Scribe and a few persons like Professor Bush and Cora Mowatt, who were deeply learned in the lore of the New Jerusalem, knew just what his message meant. Perhaps, though, there was in it some edict concerning the number of wives a man should love.

When the question was put to the Sage of Hyde Park, he delivered himself of the following sentiment: "Should a man or woman, after entering into the relation of husband and wife, become convinced by various means, that each does not embody the other's *ideal*, then they are not truly married—they are *divorced*; and both have a natural right to seek further for the embodiment of their heart's *ideal* associate. Human legislation may not forbid them to marry again. In truth, men have no right to control arbitrarily the soul's deepest, purest wants, the rights and elevations of true marriage."

This was the shortest and least ambiguous pronouncement that Andrew Jackson Davis ever made. It was taken as what Swedenborg himself would have said upon the subject had he been able to express himself in such a straightforward manner. To show their appreciation of such a courageous stand, Mary Gove and Thomas Nichols celebrated their nuptials in the Church of the New Jerusalem.

XX

"Water Cure Is Love Cure"

IN THE SPRING OF 1850 THERE AP-
PEARED IN THE NEWSPAPERS OF
NEW YORK, AND IN THE LEADING
hydropathic, mesmeristic, phrenological, Swedenborgian
and associationist journals of the country, this Card:

WATER CURE HOUSE

Thomas L. Nichols and Mary S. Gove Nichols

Water Cure Physicians,

wish to apprize their friends and the public, that they
have removed to a more eligible, convenient and
accessible residence,

No. 87 West Twenty-Second Street,

near the Sixth Avenue, in the center of the most beautiful and salubrious uptown portion of New York,
within a few minutes walks of Union, Madison, and
Grammercy parks, and only a block from the Seventh,
Broadway and Bloomingdale stages.

At this house, combining the advantages of country
air with a city residence, Dr. and Mrs. Nichols will
receive patients for full board and treatment, for day
treatment, and for consultation and examinations.
Patients also visited at their residences. Professional

[227]

visits made within a reasonable distance, and the principles of Water Cure applied to every department of medicine, surgery and obstetrics.

Letters of consultation should give a clear account of the case, with all its circumstances, and enclose a fee of five dollars. Subsequent letters, if required, one dollar.

The customary fees charged for personal consultations, examinations, visits, attendance, etc.

Hours for consultation, from 10 o'clock, A.M. to 2 o'clock P.M. Sundays excepted.

From this it might seem that Dr. and Mrs. Nichols had merely set themselves up as imitators and competitors of Dr. and Mrs. Shew. Actually by grafting upon the hydropathic technique the green shoots of Fourierism, Swedenborgianism, mesmerism, phrenology, etherology, pathetism and spiritualism, the newlyweds were able to create over on Twenty-second Street a bower more bedazzling than the simple flowering down on Bond. When explaining the difference between the Shews' establishment and their own, Mary Gove Nichols with a coyness appropriate to a bride would smirk, "To *us* Water Cure is Love Cure."

Her husband, in measured sentences that befitted one who had just been graduated near the top of his class at N.Y.U., would elaborate upon her sentiment. "Water cure as we use the term means more than giving sick people plunge baths, wet sheets, packs and douches," he would explain. "To us it comprehends a knowledge of the relation of man to the universe. It is a central science, a pivotal system, the desideratum of progress, the basis of reform, and the fulfillment of the ends of creation."

Such an all-embracing, hope-lifting science was an instant success with the intelligentsia; it also attracted a more generally solvent clientele. For the first time in her life Mary Gove felt the thrill of the encompassing arms of respectability. Mrs. Josepha Hale in her personal column in *Godey's*—which she used to instruct her subscribers about fashions, food and manners, as well as to tell her contributors just why she was refusing their offerings—recommended the new establishment in unqualified terms. Immediately carriages of intelligent and delicate *Lady's Book* fans, upon whom a Hale recommendation worked as a royal command, flocked to 87 West Twenty-second Street from the fashionable suburbs of Chelsea, Hoboken and Williamsburg, from enlightened Rhode Island and Connecticut, from progressive Ohio and Kentucky and even, a few of them, from the conservative Southern states.

No matter from where they came or how long it took them to get there, they all, according to Mrs. Nichols, brought their false virtue as well as their diseases with them. With that innate and shrinking modesty, which they considered the especial ornament of their sex, they confessed to her that they would rather die than submit to examinations needful to their cure by a male physician. Taking the hint, Thomas Nichols relieved his wife of all general practice, and the bulk of the correspondence, so that she could dedicate her full time to the exclusively female weaknesses.

As soon as she could rush the more interesting of her case histories into print—giving just enough of their backgrounds to pique the reader's curiosity about the identities of her patients—Mary Gove Nichols was generally proclaimed the most eminent authority on the female constitution and the greatest benefactress of her sex.

As a woman Mrs. Nichols was continuously amazed at the evils which chastity and indissoluble marriage had inflicted upon these ladies of charm, refinement, intellect and piety—the inspired leaders of the female prayer meetings, as well as society stars of the first magnitude. As a conscientious scientist she recorded in telling detail the maladies from which they suffered— scrofula, falling of the womb, inflammation of the uterus, pains across the back, nervous debility, painful dyspepsia, constant abortion and malignant gonorrhea.

Gross physical ailments like piles and syphilis could usually be cleared up during a three weeks' residence at the Water Cure House. Having the Priessnitzian revulsion for all condiments, Mrs. Nichols would go light on the red pepper applied to the afflicted parts— the standard treatment of the day—and have her patients sloshed about on the floor by attendants ever ready with buckets of water.

It was the mental quirks of her female patients— usually correlated with conspicuous abnormalities of the organ of amativeness—upon which Mrs. Nichols expended her ingenuity. With the aid of her husband she worked out a novel method of resolving the psychological difficulties of those who were persuaded to put their poor warped souls entirely in her hands. The Nicholses called this technique Esoteric Anthropology —a more accurately descriptive title than the later and now more generally used term Psychoanalysis. Furthermore, they knew that their methods came straight from Mesmer, a knowledge lacking in the Freudians today.

Utilizing her highly developed magnetic powers, Mrs. Nichols would extract from her entranced patients thoughts they had never before expressed to another human being—and which, in truth, they had seldom suspected themselves of thinking. When a firm clairvoyant rapprochement had been established, the docile ladies would divulge their true feelings in regard to the masculine principle, their reactions to the nocturnal behavior of their husbands, and the attraction other gentlemen had for them. As their physician artfully directed their minds back to their childhood, many would confess to highly significant secret habits.

One of the earliest and simplest cases cured by this method was that of a society star of the first magnitude. Mrs. Nichols had been but a few minutes in her presence when she was penetrated by a great sadness. There was nothing in the young woman's outward seeming to justify this sentiment. She looked not above twenty years old, her form was plump, her cheeks rosy, her complexion like the lily in fairness. Her phrenological organs were well developed, her bump of amativeness being particularly large. Yet as the feeling of sadness persisted, Mrs. Nichols turned to magnetic influence to divine the reason.

She had no sooner fixed her visitor with a loaded glance than the fair one took from her bag a little bottle of cologne, poured some upon her handkerchief and passed it over her face. A frightful pallor succeeded, and the handkerchief she held before the shocked eyes of her physician was covered with rouge.

"I am made up," said she. "I have not one tooth that is not artificial; I am bloated with porter, and am as wretchedly sick and nervous as you can ask—but just now I don't wish to speak of my general health. I am infected with a loathsome disease from my husband, who has been three months absent and says he is not to be blamed, and I suppose that he is not."

She then put her hand involuntarily in her dress pocket and drew out a letter. As she saw Mrs. Nichols' magnetic gaze fasten on the missive, her face became crimson and she burst into an agony of tears. "I can tell you *all*," said she.

"All," said Mrs. Nichols most pityingly.

"For fifteen years I have been married— Oh! how I hate that word *married*. If I had been sold at the South at fifteen, I believe I should have been less wretched. I have hated my husband since my first real knowledge of him, and yet he is not a bad man—but he is not for me. He thinks me a hysterical, sentimental fool. My antipathy to him is a feeling I can't account for, because I think him a very good man, but from my marriage day I have had a horror of sharing his bed. I would have escaped from him on any terms, if it had not been for the thought of my father and mother. He is their idol—he maintains them—he is everything to them—and I was their idol too I suppose because I was beautiful once."

"And you are still," said Mrs. Nichols.

"Mock me not," said she. "For years I have not gone to bed one night sober. I have been drunk on beer. I never could have slept with him all these years if I could not have got drunk." She seemed to have a dreadful pleasure, Mrs. Nichols noted, in using the word "drunk." "I am safe—I *know* I am safe with you. I know you will never betray me. I know you will pity me—you pity all poor, miserable married women because you know how to. Now can you do me any good?"

"Not whilst you continue to quaff beer," said Mary Gove Nichols, not letting even her sympathy overcome her Priessnitzian principles.

"Oh, if I had anything to love—if I had ever had a child to love—you do not know what it is to be utterly desolate." And again the poor creature clutched her letter.

Mrs. Nichols' clairvoyant eyes had, of course, long since grasped its significance as rightly as Miss Brackett had caught the sentiment in Colonel Stone's pictures and Andrew Jackson Davis the news in the *Tribunes* that were placed on his head. "That letter is from one you love," she declaimed.

"It is, it is," said the weeping woman. "But if scandal should taint my name, what would become of my father and mother and my young sister? Oh God! I cannot, dare not think of loving anyone, or of being saved from the life I lead. But I must be cured of this dreadful disease. My dearest friend said you could cure me. My husband told him—and he said I must come to you. I am like one on fire. I cannot tell you what I suffer in my body; my spirit suffers more—and yet as bad as I am—a drunkard"—she shuddered at the thought— "there is one that loves me—I am sure of it—and I have promised him, and I now promise you, to drink only water. Oh, he is so good, so true. He would save me for time and eternity if he could."

"Then you *are* saved," said Mrs. Nichols impulsively; then with more caution she asked, "Is your husband jealous?"

"No, oh no! If I look well in public he is satisfied; that is why I learned to paint. I saw that it was a real trouble to him when I began to lose my looks. But is it not wicked for me to love Mr. ——" and so full was her confidence that she told Mrs. Nichols the gentleman's name. "Tell me, am I a guilty woman?"

"Turn not away from this love," said Mary Gove Nichols solemnly. "It is the only sacred thing left to you."

"Water Cure Is Love Cure"

This particular lady was, of course, a push-over for the principles of esoteric anthropology, and was soon as healthy and happy as could be. The only disturbing rift in this sweet fluting of love remains the question of the dear friend's health. Obviously he had not remained inactive during the husband's three months' absence and for the husband to apprise him of his wife's illness appears unnecessary. Was the fair one cured only to be sent back to the source of infection? Mrs. Nichols does not say, but goes on to further cases.

Those who needed particularly subtle treatment were the leaders of the female prayer meetings, the majority of whom delighted their analyst by confessing to long addiction to the solitary vice, and matrons who after long years of marriage still declared boastfully that they were as chaste as ice and had never felt the slightest temptation to the masculine principle. The phrenological charts of all those who expressed such unnatural and diseased sentiments showed without exception serious derangements of the organs of amativeness. To such a one Mrs. Nichols would say tenderly:

"My dear, your nervous system is drained of life. It is not natural for a woman to be without amative passion. It is a great wrong in her nature when she is deprived of the wish and power of amative pleasure. Diseased amativeness results in the atonic condition which is termed wrongly virtue and purity in women."

If at this point in the analysis the patient bowed her head in tears and deep humiliation, Mrs. Nichols would know that she wasn't so hopelessly diseased at all. She hadn't been deprived by nature of an itch for the masculine principle; she had simply been married to the wrong man. Her agitation proved that she was now ready for an exposition of the general principles upon which esoteric anthropology was built.

"A woman's highest duty as well as her most sacred right," Mrs. Nichols would explain, "is to *herself*. If she continues to give her body to the pollution of a so-called indissoluble marriage, to a sexual union in which she knows no pleasure, then she is guilty of a great sin and a horrible impurity. By the standards of the Higher Law of Health and Purity, which is as high as the sky above the contemptibly low laws of man, she must be judged a convenient harlot, a legal prostitute."

If now the agitated lady asked humbly, "But can I be cured of this impurity?" Mrs. Nichols was ready to move on to a crucial phase of the analysis—getting the co-operation of the husband. She asked permission to examine his head.

If the phrenological test proved his functions of self-sacrifice and well-meaningness to be well developed, Mrs. Nichols seldom had any difficulty in persuading him to protect his wife while she freely bestowed both her love and her person on the particular other gentleman who was always in the offing. Thus the lady's sinless happiness restored her organ of amativeness to normal proportions.

Should the phrenological examination of the husband

show him to possess the qualities of stupidity, ill-meaningness and hatefulness to a conspicuous degree, Mrs. Nichols was prepared for trouble. A man of such low mentality could not understand the finer principles of esoteric anthropology. Instead of co-operating in his wife's cure, he would vulgarly complain that her physician was encouraging her to commit adultery. To such a self-seeking charge Mrs. Nichols would reply with a logic familiar to all liberals, "It is her union with *you* that is adulterous, for you know not the meaning of purity." And to the wife she would give this counsel:

"Show your utter contempt and abhorrence of this gluttonous man and the false laws he has unconsciously adopted. Cease any longer to be a drudge to his isolate household, ministering to the base in his brain. Refuse any longer to be his legal prostitute. Get a divorce if possible, but if this is denied, live your own true, pure and loving life, as far as disgrace, poverty and persecution will allow you to do so."

XXI

The Intellectuals Look at Marriage

IT HAPPENED NOT INFREQUENTLY THAT A HUSBAND CAUGHT THE IDEA BEHIND ESOTERIC ANTHROPOLOGY more quickly than his wife. This circumstance led Mrs. Nichols to a statement bitterly resented by orthodox women's righters: "The evils of indissoluble marriage are by no means confined to woman. They reflect upon man whilst the union continues with terrible powers that can never be reckoned."

In such cases Mrs. Nichols would usually decide that the wife was too far gone in the pollution of chastity to be cured, but that the husband must be saved. She would then bend her energies to liberating him from the impurities of a passionless union. It was a case of this sort which brought the Nicholses their most interesting friendship, the consequences of which were not inconsiderable upon the intellectual life of the early 1850's.

A lady of the finest intellect, most devoted piety, great fascination and charm of manner and qualities, but delicate and weak in health, came to Twenty-second Street for a consultation. As was to be expected from the atonic condition of her organ of amativeness, she confessed that while she loved her husband most tenderly she had felt a lessening of sensual attraction toward him.

"He is a man of great strength and delicacy and beauty of character," said she, "who after twenty years of marriage still respects my slightest wish. As yet he is perfectly faithful to the bond of marriage, but unfortunately has not been delivered by God from the temptation to youthful amative indulgence."

So intelligent was this lady that her treatment got off to a fine start. When Mrs. Nichols explained that from what she said her husband was probably a true, pure and natural human being, while she herself was false and evil, she got the idea at a glance. "I see the whole wide web of wrong and injustice I have done my noble husband," said she, weeping bitterly, "yet I still feel an inability to stem his amative want."

Mrs. Nichols then suggested, quite reasonably, she thought, that the lady allow her husband to love another, and another, and yet another; if so many could be found worthy of so great a love.

At this there burst from the hitherto charming lady "such a bitter selfishness, such a power of bigotry, such an unreasoning and unhuman feeling of arbitrary personal property"—that Mrs. Nichols summoned the husband for an immediate consultation. His examination disclosed a more perfect phrenological development than is found in many thousand; one of the best her age had the good fortune to produce. This was not altogether surprising for the cranium which Mrs. Nichols had been fingering contained the staggeringly encyclopedic brain of Stephen Pearl Andrews, who held a special place among the liberals of the middle nineteenth century.

Since he was a native of Massachusetts and the son of a preacher, Stephen Pearl Andrews had opened his predestined eyes on the spectacle of the Southern Negro. When at nineteen and just out of Amherst he began to inveigh against slavery, his voice might have been lost among the chorus of other Northern young men crying the same tune, except that instead of preaching abolition to sympathetic New Englanders, he carried his message to the dandies of New Orleans and the planters who were settling the new free State of Texas.

The Louisianans paid little attention to his exhortations, but the Texans took them seriously enough to burn his house and send him running. Hallowed by this experience, he arrived at the International Anti-slavery Convention of 1843 to become the star of the show.

These international abolitionist meetings—held intermittently in London from 1833, when Britain bought off the slaves in her colonies for 20,000,000 pounds, until ours were set free in a more liberal manner—were the biggest things in the lives of the Americans who could afford to attend them. The meeting now best known was that held in 1840, for that was the one at which William Lloyd Garrison did *not* make a speech. He deprived the Londoners of his thunder in retaliation for their refusal to allow Lucretia Mott and Elizabeth Stanton to harangue the male delegates—an event duly commemorated when these ladies' husbands organized the Women's Rights Party.

Though the convention of 1840 has taken on an historical importance in the tradition of liberalism, it was the one held three years later that seemed much more exciting at the time. Its sessions were attended not only by the usual boatloads of wealthy Tappans and eloquent Channings from America but by some of England's most influential statesmen. And none other than Stephen Pearl Andrews was responsible for the gracious presence of Lord Aberdeen, Lord Russell and Lord Palmerston among the awed pilgrims from America.

His coat-tails still smoking from the fire-brands of the Texans, Andrews upon arrival in London had gone straight to see Aberdeen, who was Peel's Foreign Secretary. He proposed to him that His Majesty's Government free the slaves of Texas on the same cash basis that it had bought off those in the Indies. In return, Andrews promised that Texas would henceforth consider Britain, and not the United States, its lawful protector.

Aberdeen, who had never held the common British abhorrence of the Holy Alliance and who as a consequence had scant respect for the Monroe Doctrine, considered buying off a few thousand blacks a cheap way of getting a foothold on the American Continent. He warmed to Andrews' proposal and sent word to his Chargé d'Affaires in Texas to make preparations for the deal. When the message was relayed to the Texans, it was met with indignation. Andrews could not speak for the Free State and, besides, the planters were in the market for more slaves, rather than for selling those they had.

When Edward Everett got wind of these arnoldish goings-on he reluctantly—because the American minister to London was himself a New Englander and therefore loath to rat on his fellow abolitionists—informed Washington about the "mare's nest" Andrews had stirred up. President Tyler and his Cabinet were as sore as the Texans. The two groups of slave-mongers got together and as a result Texas joined not England but the United States.

Since the annexation of Texas was the precipitating cause of the Mexican War, many liberals in after years maintained that to Stephen Pearl Andrews, rather than to William Lloyd Garrison, belonged the distinction of being the first American reformer to cause blood to flow over the question of slavery.

Having pursued his abolitionism to an international impasse, Andrews turned his versatile mind to another problem. Like sufferers from dementia præcox, liberals too are concerned with words as words. When they talk or write they every now and then discover that they are using the identical tools for their cerebrations as a Tory or an ordinary person. Whenever this happens, the liberal sets himself down to give everyday words a twist that only he and his fellows can follow. This compulsion hit Andrews, just as it hits others of today, as a novel idea.

Learning while he was in England that Isaac Pitman had evolved a system of shorthand in which certain definite vocal sounds were represented by certain definite symbols, Andrews saw in this phonography a means of putting over his semantics. Consequently, after taking the requisite number of lessons, he sailed for Boston where he established the first Pitman School in America.

But alas! Boston took shorthand then as shorthand is taken today—merely as an aid to business—and Andrews came down to New York to get on with his Universology. This work was to be the distillation of all the world's knowledge acquired by him, he said with a fine disdain of Grimm's Law, from a familiarity with thirty-three distinct and unrelated languages. The twenty-year labor when finally published could be understood, the author boasted, by only seven other persons—a fair percentage of customer interest when one learns that less than twenty copies of Universology were disposed of.

Andrews was still at work on pre-Christian thought —extracting the basic similarities between Chinese wisdom and Hindu mysticism—when fate in the strange guise of his wife's diseased amativeness brought him the intensely sympathetic friendship of Mary Gove Nichols. At her insistence he added to his already weighty load of ancient knowledge an understanding of all the modern doctrines that had gone into the making of esoteric anthropology. When his mentor disclosed to him that it was from her study of associationism that she had derived her certainty that what his wife regarded as mere goatishness in him was really the purest and holiest of impulses, Stephen Pearl Andrews declared with novel modesty that Fourier was the most remarkable genius that had ever lived.

He was therefore hurt and indignant when he read in the literary section of the Sunday *Tribune* a very saucy and superficial review of Elsworth Lazarus' *Love and Marriage and Passional Hygiene*. To make things even harder to take, the review was signed by that supposedly orthodox liberal, Henry James.

Andrews was not the only intellectual in New York to be stunned by the seeming violence of James' attack on the Lazarus book which, though it contained large hunks of mesmerism, Swedenborgianism, physiology, and anatomy, and lesser bits on wine-growing, masturbation, birth control, French poetry and abortion, was, or at least so far as anyone could make out, Fourieristic in its treatment of love and marriage.

This was the second book to be printed in America since Brisbane introduced associationism to his countrymen which put more emphasis on Fourier's sexual theories than his economic dreams. The first had been an anonymous translation of *Love in the Phalansteries* written by one of Fourier's few French followers, Victor Hannequin.

With a vision as far-seeing as Fourier or Brisbane, but in a more comprehensible style, Hannequin pictured the love life of the world once all of us were neatly housed in associations. Love was going to be definitely free. Monogamy would not be abolished, but neither would it be encouraged. The medieval Court of Love would be dug up and the seraglio moved over. And that "noble and powerful type of generous women," who had so long been outcasts from society, would come into their own. No longer would they be mercenary profligates degraded to making a trade of love. Under the fancy names of Bayarderes and Bacchantes they would be exalted and honored for the "impassioned industry with which they pursued their attractive labors." In the phalansteries of the future special pains would be taken to satisfy two other groups whose desires must too often remain unsated in this imperfect world: old men who horsed after fresh young virgins and aging women who burned for virile young men. The earth would be searched for wolf-bait necessary to appease these neglected and often abused "minorities."

The translator of these amorous visions not only approved them warmly in a preface almost as long as Hannequin's tract, but expressed his own personal convictions by stating that wherever "mutual preference of each other exists between the parties, there Love exists, and in a true social order every expression of it would be divinely and beautifully sacred." Though the author of these sentiments tried to keep his identity secret, every well-informed person in New York and New England knew that he was Henry James.

Dr. Lazarus in his *Love and Marriage and Passional Hygiene* had repeated the same lofty convictions about the sacred beauty of "variety" in love. He naturally expected James to give his book a whooping send-off and was deeply hurt by his abuse.

Stephen Pearl Andrews, who was more used to controversy than meek Elsworth Lazarus, was indignant. He wrote angrily to Greeley, upbraiding him for allowing James in the pages of the *Tribune* to mock the associationist cause in which all true liberals must believe. Greeley, who prided himself upon having in his Sunday book section the most enlightened literary organ of the day, was delighted that one of his reviewers was causing so much excitement. Being himself less familiar with the amorous phases of Fourierism than with its social implications, he suggested to James and Andrews that they conduct in the columns of the *Tribune* a thorough discussion of the proper status of "Love, Marriage and Divorce" in a more perfect society. Greeley would serve as "impartial umpire."

Andrews, fresh from his conversion to the breath-taking vision of universal free love, waded right in and repeated the sentiments he had learned from the Nicholses. Celibacy, he proclaimed, was more unnatural than sodomy or bestiality; constancy between a husband and wife more degrading than prostitution. Marriage as the world now knew it must be abolished.

Henry James took a more temperate and philosophic stand, as befitted one who had given long thought to the problem under discussion. The conclusion at which he arrived was the result not of the *Tribune* symposium alone but of a twenty-five-year search for a philosophy by which he could adjust himself perfectly and simultaneously to the impulses of his own body, the restrictions of society, the laws of nature and the will of God. The search had begun when James was sent to Union College by his father who had underwritten that institution to the extent of $100,000 out of respect for the piety of its aging president, Eliphalet Nott.

XXII

Henry James, John Humphrey Noyes and the Perfectionists

ELIPHALET NOTT HAD NOT ALLOWED HIS ORTHODOX CALVINISM TO IN-TERFERE WITH HIS INTEREST IN the great scientific and social movements of the day. Indeed he had found, like many another divine—notably John Pierpont and LaRoy Sunderland—that an aptitude for explaining the simple miracles of the Bible was a fine preparation for accepting the fancier miracles of mesmerism and water cure; and that persuading young bucks to join temperance unions and wayward daughters to join Magdalen societies gave one the proper experience for persuading the whole world to submit to the newest ideas about social reorganization.

President Nott's ability to combine the old with the new, and his belief that while getting himself acceptable for heaven a man was duty-bound to improve his fellow beings and the earth upon which they temporarily dwelt, had already caused Union's three most distinguished graduates, Thomas Brownell, Francis Wayland and John Worth Edmonds, to become outstanding liberals of the day. His influence upon young Henry James was just as great.

[248]

Like Wayland and Brownell, James showed his adoration of Nott's teachings by deciding to become a preacher, himself. He was already in his second year at the Princeton Theological Seminary when he was struck by a devastating doubt concerning the absolute literalness of the early chapters of Genesis. Was the story of the Creation, he wondered, founded upon verifiable scientific fact? Was it the exact history of the human race? Perhaps. And then again it might be something quite different and much more splendid—"a symbolic revelation of God's own spiritual creation and providence."

Unable to keep such thoughts from tearing at his mind, James felt compelled to quit the seminary. He did so abruptly, believing himself to be the most spiritually lonely young man in the country.

Once away from Princeton and working as a newspaper reporter in Boston, however, he found himself in a goodly company of similar revolutionary thinkers. Indeed, in the early 1830's it was almost as common for young men who had been reared on Calvin and Jonathan Edwards to revolt against the doctrines of total depravity and infant damnation as it was for those who, like Albert Brisbane, had been brought up on Jefferson and Thomas Paine to revolt against what they termed the cold atheism of their fathers.

The universalist doctrine that the entire human race could and must be saved from its predilection to sin and disbelief was as intoxicating to the one group of révoltés as to the other. But those in whom Calvinism was so ingrained that they could not bring themselves to a belief in a completely sinless universe, found a more satisfactory drink in Finney's insistence that if a man contritely confessed his own sins and publicly professed his belief in Jesus Christ then, no matter if the rest of the world did keep on sliding into Hell, he himself would stand a pretty sure chance of getting into Heaven —providing of course that he did not backslide in the interval between his conversion and Judgment Day.

That backsliding was the big problem for all those who believed in an exclusively personal and individual salvation, taking place against a world growing constantly more temptingly evil. It kept many converts confessing and professing almost continuously. Others sought to solve the problem more practically by hastening the day of Judgment.

William Miller, an upstate New York farmer with a license to preach to the Baptists, re-read the Scriptures and discovered that Christ would return to judge the quick and the dead in the year 1843. His thousands of followers throughout New York and New England were so heartened by the thought of having to wait only a few years for their heavenly reward that they quit work, sold their possessions, bought their ascension robes, said a pitying good-by to the skeptical acquaintances whom they would never see again, and waited exultantly for the upward lift. When the great day arrived and passed and they found themselves still earth-bound, the bitterest part of the disappointment was having to accept the skeptical ones' bounty while re-establishing themselves in the world as it is.

A man of Henry James' complicated mentality and background could not of course find much sustenance in the crude prophecies of Adventist Miller. But he was attracted to the not altogether different but decidedly more learned doctrine of Perfectionism. The original Perfectionist was John Humphrey Noyes who had been pondering theology at Andover and Yale during the years that James was at Union and Princeton.

His academic background enabled Noyes to make a much more profound study of the Second Coming than the self-taught Miller, and to arrive at a far more impressive date. The Adventists, as well as the more conventional Christians, were all wrong according to Noyes' calculations in looking *forward* to the Judgment Day. They should look back.

The memorable event had already occurred centuries before—in the year 70 A.D., to be exact. And every person who after that time had got the true religion was automatically saved for eternity. The trouble was that from 70 to 1837 no living man had got the true religion. In the latter year John Humphrey Noyes rectified conditions. After spending several weeks in the brothels of the Five Points, he delivered himself of a whopping confession and announced that he had become Perfect. Henceforth and for eternity he would be without sin and above man-made laws. He also proposed to make

Saints out of all those who would conscientiously follow his teachings.

The article in the Perfectionist doctrine that was of particular interest to Henry James had to do with the relationship between the sexes. Friction of any kind was painful to him, and the household naggings that occurred within the bonds of matrimony particularly unbearable. He thought therefore that Noyes might be getting close to the source of human evils when he proclaimed that "when the will of God is done on earth as it is in heaven, there will be no marriage." Elaborating this idea further, the great Perfectionist declared:

"The marriage supper of the Lamb is a feast at which every dish is free to every guest. Exclusiveness, jealousy, quarreling, have no place there, for the same reason as that which forbids the guests at a thanksgiving dinner to claim each his separate dish, and quarrel with the rest for his rights. In a holy community there is no more reason why sexual intercourse should be restrained by law, than why eating and drinking should be; and there is as little occasion for shame in the one case as in the other. . . . I call a certain woman my wife— she is yours; she is Christ's and in Him she is the bride of all saints. She is dear in the hand of a stranger and according to my promise to her I rejoice."

By the time he became familiar with Perfectionism— now hallowed in the annals of liberalism as the first philosophy to contain a concept of free love that stemmed entirely from native American roots—James had progressed so far in worrying over the fate of man-kind in general that he could no longer experience the essentially personal emotion that is necessary to conversion to any Christian sect, no matter how bizarre its tenets. Also it seems that his curiosity about communal sexuality might have been truly philosophic and idealistic. At any rate, he took only one wife—and there is no record of any extensive research at the Five Points— and after he came into his share of his father's estate bought a one-family dwelling at 41 Washington Square in New York City.

There his two sons, William and Henry, Junior, were born. There, as to a spiritual oasis, repaired the really high-class thinkers of New England—Emerson, Thoreau, Theodore Parker and Bronson Alcott—when fat lecture fees lured them to the crass and materialistic metropolis. In extended conversations with these congenially serious souls, and alone in his study, James pondered without ceasing the great questions concerning the ultimate relationships of society, nature and God.

Such preoccupation inevitably brought on the disease which wealthy young men of the period seemed unable to escape—"over-worked brain." Like his predecessors James took a sea voyage as a treatment. The atmosphere of the Atlantic helped temporarily, but the materialistic air of London had an even worse effect on him than that of Paris had on Albert Brisbane. It gave psychic configuration to his malady.

The Mad Forties

In his calmest moments, sitting with his family over the evening meal, his mind would be attacked by "some damned shape squatting invisible to me within the precincts of the room, and raying out from his fetid personality influences fatal to life."

The English doctor he consulted recommended water cure, but hydropathy in England in 1844 had not reached the high intellectual level it attained in America after the Nicholses really went to work on it. Spiritually the British water cures were not much different from Saratoga and the White Sulphur Springs.

James' body was put into wet sheets and wet girdles and sitz baths, but nothing was done to his mind. The loathsome, deadly, invisible shape followed him even into the douche room. Yet his visit to that British water cure was the turning point in his life. While enduring its dampness he met a woman who did not think the detestable, raying creature who was his constant companion was at all strange.

Mrs. Chichester thought James was rather blessed. Why, it was a "vastation," she said—the very same experience that Emanuel Swedenborg had undergone. When pressed for details, she recommended Garth Wilkinson in London, who was attempting to collect and translate the Swedenborg manuscripts which had been neglected for almost a century. Not waiting to redampen his girdle James hurried up to town. As under Wilkinson's happy tutelage he began to comprehend the Divine Mind and the Spiritual Spheres, the squatting creature quit him in disgust.

Henry James' finicky soul had at last experienced the exaltation it had so long been seeking, one which the most eloquent of American evangelists had not been able to touch off. Contemplating Swedenborg's exceedingly complicated celestial universe, he was "lifted by a sudden miracle into felt harmony with universal man and filled to the brim with the sentiment of indestructible life."

He naturally wanted to impose his new vision upon others and take them with him into an unfamiliar world. He was surprised, though not dismayed, to find that those few Englishmen who had so much as heard of Swedenborg dismissed his theories as being merely crackpot. Granted Swedenborg was insane, James retorted, remembering that loathsome, squatting figure, what possible bearing could that have on the veracity of his revelations? Was profound metaphysical truth to be discounted just because the man who first proclaimed it happened to be out of his mind?

The English preoccupation and satisfaction with the world as it was made James long for the more congenial atmosphere of America. So grabbing a load of Swedenborgian works, which were less numerous but certainly no less obscure than the library Alcott had lugged back the year before, Henry James came home. By the time he landed, his bundle of books had become his most precious possession, the real core of his being.

He never after that got beyond reach of them, even toting them along when he went visiting. They became the materialization of his old psychic configuration; the incubus that was to lay the best minds of New England.

Emerson opened his arms to the philosopher he had admired so greatly at second and third hand. He made such good use of his friend's books that his lecture "Swedenborg: the Mystic" was soon more popular than "Spurzheim: the Scientist." In return, he introduced James to the colonists at Brook Farm, just then embarking upon water cure and associationism.

Emerson stayed at Brook Farm only on week-ends, but he faithfully followed the Priessnitzian diet at his own table. And he turned his Concord home into a miniature phalanx by imposing menial "tasks of necessity" upon himself and insisting that his servants eat with the family and join in the exalted conversations. These conversations paralleled closely those taking place at West Roxbury and the more cultured gatherings in New York.

Since the Emerson servants, for all the urging they had to participate freely in the discussions, were for the most part tongue-tied in the presence of the master, the interplay of ideas at Concord was usually as harmonious as any Fourierist could wish. Conversations at Brook Farm and in New York were by contrast too often agitated by an unphilosophic, all-too-human lack of calm. Such controversies turned on the question concerning the comparative greatness of Charles Fourier and

Emanuel Swedenborg and their plans for saving the universe.

Everyone agreed that with the possible exception of Jesus Christ, those two had attained the highest phrenological development ever reached by immortal man. Certainly their plans for the social and spiritual reorganization of the cosmos were more elaborate, and therefore more workable, than the simple rules laid down by the Nazarene. Yet it could not be denied that in many practical metaphysical particulars these plans were dissimilar.

There was, as a simple example, the problem of numerology. Both philosophers scorned such simple numbers as one and two. Yet Swedenborg, accepting the geo-political concept of heaven, earth and hell, did not doubt that a completely acceptable universe could be based on multiples of the number Three. Fourier, on the other hand, with his constant distrust of all symbols that might be tainted by existing thought, shied off from the trinitarian concepts too often associated with Christian theology and Greek philosophy. He dug far into the Oriental past and came up with the Lenox Avenue number of Seven as the most practical one around which to build the new social order.

Then, too, there was the problem of the place of animals in a better world. Swedenborg, like Mrs. Mowatt, wanted special beneficence shown to the lowliest of God's creatures; the more loathsome the brute, the greater the divine subsidy. Fourier, though he ap-

proved of reviving such extinct Oriental and imaginary
beasts as the Anka and the Butta, wanted to exclude
several still extant species from his brave new cosmos.
His plan called for a purge of all caterpillars, who
represented civilization to him, and of doves, whom he
associated with the detested twosome.

In other essential details did these two systems of
thought differ. So the great question about which the
planners in New York and West Roxbury argued continuously was this: Which of these two absolutely true
interpretations of the universe was the truest?

Since it was impossible ever to answer that question,
it became imperative to reconcile and compound the two
great guides to the better life into one absolute and non-
contradictory blue print of the future. To this herculean
task Henry James, George Ripley, Parke Godwin,
Charles W. Dana, William Henry Channing and Henry
Calvert dedicated their intellects. They decided to
found a magazine in which they could apprise the public of their consolidating thoughts as soon as they were
birthed. *New Times* was to be its name and James its
editor-in-chief. The first issued was never printed.

Within one week of thinking about thinking, their
task had become even more stupendous than the thinkers
had foreseen. Since the new all-over philosophy must
preserve everything that was worth preserving, Goethe's
loftiest sentiments, so Dana pointed out, must somehow
be worked into it. Channing was just as sure that the
principles enunciated by Priessnitz must not be omitted,

while Calvert insisted that the theories of Gall and Mesmer would have to be rung in. Only Henry James refused to be diverted by these secondary issues.

In comparing the theories of Swedenborg and Fourier, he found one subject on which the two were in agreement not only with one another but with John Humphrey Noyes. All three were alike in insisting that in a more perfect world a substitute must be found for conventional marriage. It was this discovery that caused James to translate and preface so enthusiastically *Love in the Phalansteries*. Soon he had a chance to weigh his vision of free love against its practical application.

In 1848 Noyes took a select group of his saints to a farm near Oneida, New York, and set up a colony free from the laws of less perfect men. In this community of the Lord every dish was as free as it supposedly was in Heaven. No generous hearted woman was degraded into cashing in on her generosity. And particular attention was paid to mating virgins to old men, and virile youths with older women wise in the ways of Eros. Henry James went to have a look. He expected to be elated; he was shocked.

Free love as practiced at Oneida was not the divinely attractive, joyously beautiful relationship that Fourier and Hannequin had foreseen. The indiscriminate mating of the Perfectionists was just as "strenuous" and every bit as "unhandsome" as the coupling of cattle. The dishes were free enough, but they were most certainly not Sèvres. Their communal experience brought the Oneida colonists no deeper understanding of all mankind, no compelling tolerance, no exquisite tenderness. It left them harder, James decided, and meaner and more bigoted Calvinists than they had been before.

He returned to New York with a new respect for the institution of marriage. It was in that reactionary mood that he reviewed Elsworth Lazarus' book. By the time of the *Tribune* symposium, however, he had somewhat regained his broader social outlook. Though he still held that under certain special conditions monogamy could be a not entirely unpleasant experience, he agreed with Andrews that in a better world divorce should be made instantaneous. He agreed further that until the court of love was revived and the seraglio brought westward, commercial prostitution was a necessary institution of society.

XXIII

Women to the Fore

HORACE GREELEY WAS GENUINELY DISTRESSED BY THE TURN HIS SYMPOSIUM ON SEX MORALS IN A changing world had taken. When at its beginning he had announced grandly that while he might disagree with James and Andrews on a few minor points he courted a free expression of their opinions, he had no idea that these opinions would be so completely twentieth century. Indeed during the ten years that the *Tribune* had been bounding into solvency and influence, Greeley had been much too busy with practical affairs to realize how preoccupied his fellow associationists had become with sex.

When at the beginning of his friendship with Brisbane he had proclaimed Fourier as a liberator of woman he had done so under the impression that associationism would rescue her from the kitchen, not deliver her to the brothel. While still holding that some of Fourier's ideas might prove beneficial to labor, Greeley felt that he owed it to his more conservative readers to make his own stand on sexual manners completely clear—because, after all, it would be himself, not Andrews or

James, who would suffer most if these readers, whipped on by their parsons, abruptly canceled their subscriptions. Accordingly he re-affirmed in no uncertain terms his own unshakable belief in the absolute indissolubility of all marriages and declared flatly that should such "indissolubility be overthrown it would result in a general profligacy and corruption such as this country has never known and few of our people can adequately imagine." The ensuing "levity" would be so widespread and unrestrained that "every innocent young maiden would be sought in marriage by those who now plot her ruin without marriage."

This forthright statement restored Greeley's reputation for right thinking with the bulk of his subscribers. But for abandoning his self-chosen role of "impartial umpire" Stephen Pearl Andrews called him "unfair, tricky and mean" and implied clearly that his side was robbed. To which Greeley replied that Mr. Andrews was himself "eminently detestable."

Yet after this flare-up of acrimony had died down Greeley was loath to let the symposium end—especially after discovering that instead of cutting down on circulation, New Yorkers had found the *Tribune's* imaginary descriptions of love in a perfect world as good reading as the equally imaginative details in the *Herald's* ever fresh murders on the lower west side. Finally he decided how the discussion could be kept alive and at the same time elevated.

Though he and James and Andrews agreed on hardly

anything else, they did agree that should marriage laws be liberalized and sexual morals made more free, women just in the nature of things stood to lose or benefit more by the change than men. Why not then ask a representative modern woman to present her views on sex for the kind of world in which she wished her children to live? It would make a nice publicity tie-up with the Women's Rights Party convening at the Broadway Tabernacle, to have an officer of that organization state her views on whether divorce should be made easier.

The indignation aroused in the hearts of American abolitionists over the snubbing the Londoners had given Mrs. Mott and Mrs. Stanton back in 1840 had within a dozen years produced a national movement—dedicated not only to seeing to it that determined American women could talk at anti-slavery gatherings as long-windedly as they desired, but that they should also have the right to vote for abolitionist candidates in political elections and eventually to reduce the Southern majority in Congress by themselves becoming Senators and Representatives.

Women talked so much at the Party meetings and prayed so fervently and argued so tempestuously that many of them forgot that the Women's Rights movement had actually been inaugurated by men. At the New York convention Lucy Stone, looking mistily back to the day five years before when "as a mere handful of friends we met in Central New York," recollected happily "that meeting was presided over by the President of this Convention—Mrs. Mott." To which Mrs. Mott modestly replied, "I must ask leave to make a correction. The president of the meeting adverted to was not Mrs. Mott, but Mrs. Mott's husband."

James Mott, who had given up his business in order to promote Lucretia—written her speeches, taught her to read and recite them, and protected her from the feathered friends of the hoodlums—was willing to become "Mrs. Mott's husband." Henry Stanton and Samuel Blackwell accepted the same obscurity so that Elizabeth Cady and Antoinette Brown could shine. But William Lloyd Garrison had not given his support to the movement just to allow his womenfolk to show off.

The number of offices connected with the Party was prodigious, and in successive years Mrs. Mott, Mrs. Stanton, Miss Stone, the Reverend Miss Brown, the aging Grimke girls, Susan Anthony, Lydia Fowler, Madame Aneka and the other hard-working sisters were elected to first one and then another of them. But as by royal prerogative William Lloyd Garrison held on to his title of First Vice President. The ladies presided over the conventions, kept the records, collected the dues and offered the resolutions. John Pierpont, William Henry Channing and Orson Fowler made the high-brow formal addresses. William Lloyd Garrison controlled the minds and emotions of the delegates. At every meeting he exhorted them, and always on the single theme that obsessed him—"the cursed and polluted South."

Whenever some minister of the Methodist Church would cut in on his denunciations to inquire mildly what bearing the depravity of the South could have upon the problem of securing educational opportunities and property rights for the women of the North, Garrison would hurl at the "utterly useless individual" his favorite epithets—blackguard and rowdy. The lady officers, caught up in the frenzy, would demand in their New England accents that the bum be thrown out.

The ladies became so used to hearing abolition and women's rights extolled together that they identified themselves with the black people of the South. Lucy Stone declared, "I do abhor with an abhorrence I cannot express" female colleges such as Mrs. Willard's because in her mind they were indistinguishable from the slave galleries in Southern churches. Before the North had won a single engagement in the Civil War, Elizabeth Stanton and Susan Anthony had drawn up a hole-proof plan for winning the peace by forcing a one way passage to Liberia, on the day of the armistice, upon every white male born south of Wilmington.

Such violent sectionalism endeared these ladies to Mr. Garrison, but it did not give them the philosophic calm which Mr. Greeley required of the representative who would present the modern woman's case in the *Tribune*. Calmer souls were not easily found in the high councils of the feminists. Sophisticated, accomplished women like Mrs. Willard, Mrs. Hale and Mrs. Shew avoided the women's righters as they did the denizens of the Points and the Hook, and as instinctively. They were fully conscious of their very real superiority over mere males, and they had no idea of turning it in for some vague, tiresome political equality.

By 1850 the women of America wielded a power which had never before been equaled at any time or in any other country. In industry and commerce they were still confined to the looms and the notion counters, but in the higher spheres they were at the top. They edited the magazines, managed the philanthropies, controlled the churches, and governed society. When it came to morals they were supreme. As Mrs. Shew was so fond of saying, "It is our business to make men better and theirs to strengthen us for the task. Woman's love, purified and made wise, is to be the sick and sinful world's redemption." No woman with a grain of sense would relinquish the moral security such thoughts engendered for the opportunity of being pushed around at the polls by Tammany politicians and their slatternly wives.

So the literary ladies of America stayed away from the Women's Rights conventions in omnibus loads. There were only two exceptions—Mrs. Gage of St. Louis and Mrs. Elizabeth Oakes Smith. Although the homey recitations of "Aunt Fanny, the Poet"—as Mrs. Gage was known affectionately to her sisters—were great features of the conventions, her prose showed traces of illiteracy and weak-mindedness. Mrs. Oakes Smith was of a different caliber. She was the author of "The Sinless Child," a poem that had produced as many tears as "The Raven" had shudders, and she was one of the most high-brow members of the Literati.

When, after becoming famous, she moved down to New York she joined the Women's Righters under the impression that the rights toward which they were striving were those same vague, lofty privileges about which John Neal had spoken so beautifully back in Maine, and was rewarded immediately with a vice presidency. It was she whom Horace Greeley selected to present the modern woman's thoughts on "Love, Marriage and Divorce." Her learned dissertation was a great disappointment to those who expected spicy revelations from an officer of the Women's Rights Party.

She used her allotted columns to discuss all the irrelevant subjects that interested her, and especially to reassure those who were fearful that the franchise would coarsen womanhood. Not at all, declared Mrs. Oakes Smith. "Woman's touch" was the very thing that "world affairs" needed most urgently. Not the touch, to be sure, of those painted and padded wastrels who flitted and flirted at Saratoga, Newport and the White Sulphur. The type of woman who would deceive the world about her own face and figure would no doubt stoop to worse deceits in politics. The woman that Elizabeth Oakes Smith visualized as uplifting world affairs through her ballot was a combination of Sappho,

Joan of Arc, Madame de Stael and the author of "The Sinless Child and Other Poems." When she reluctantly turned her learned essay to the problem under discussion and faced the question of whether easier divorces were desirable, "Good heavens," she wrote, "no!!! They are becoming the disgrace of the country."

This effusion satisfied few of the *Tribune's* readers, and Stephen Pearl Andrews not at all. He told Mr. Greeley that to get a woman's view of love and divorce expressed cogently he would have to go outside the Women's Rights clique and select a representative of the sex who combined those "wonderful intuitions of the spiritual sphere of woman with a truly masculine strength and understanding of general principles." In his and Mr. Greeley's own set there was just such a person—" a noble and pure-minded woman, to whom the world owes more than any other man or woman, living or dead." Her name, of course, was Mary Gove Nichols. Since Mrs. Hale in her recently published monumental study of "Woman's Record" from Biblical times until the present had described Mrs. Nichols in words just about as superlative, Horace Greeley was agreeable. Mrs. Nichols rose grandly to the occasion.

She improved on her own oft repeated statement that a loveless marriage was as bad as prostitution. She now estimated that it was a million times worse, because "in a house of infamy there is one chance in a million that persons may meet who are in some measure congenial." With one deft, surgical stroke she cut through all the twaddle concerning women's rights: "If a woman has any right in this world it is the right to her own ovum." And as for indissoluble marriage—which she preferred to call by the correct name of "lawful whoredom"—if Mr. Greeley wanted really to understand what it was, then let him visit the medical museum at Albany. There in a large cabinet he would find the world's finest exposition of indissoluble marriages—rows of glass vases filled to bursting with uterine tumors. She ended her scientific dissertation by asking Mr. Greeley this direct and pertinent question:

"Suppose a woman loved seven men in turn, had a child by each, and *continued* to love them, what hurt is that to you? Would the loving union of one man with seven women—and of one woman with seven men—would this true and noble love be a curse to *you*?"

Horace Greeley did not answer her question. Neither did he print her article. He returned it with the information that it was "indecent," "licentious," "scandalous," and "unfit for the columns of my paper." And he brought the entire symposium to an abrupt close. He would not extend it long enough to allow Mrs. Oakes Smith to defend herself against subscribers who, exercising the reader's immemorial right to misinterpret a writer's stand on any controversial subject, sent indignant letters to the *Tribune* chiding her for painting her face, padding her bosom and ditching her husbands. Mrs. Oakes Smith wrote in her autobiography that Mr. Greeley's unchivalrous treatment of her on this occasion was just what she should have expected from a man who kept on his hat, put his feet on the table, and spat on the carpet in ladies' drawing rooms.

Mrs. Oakes Smith's diary remains in manuscript until this day, but Mrs. Gove Nichols' attacks on Horace Greeley were printed immediately and repetitiously in the house organ of the Twenty-second Street Water Cure House. She adopted the familiar liberal dodge of ascribing to her opponent the very same shortcomings of which she herself had been accused. "Mr. Greeley's alleged purity—Purity Bah!!!" she shouted in each issue of *Nichols' Journal*, was nothing more than a mask for his own low sex morals.

Mary Gove Nichols' animosity was directed entirely against Greeley, and she lashed at him as fiercely as she had learned to do at Hiram Gove. Stephen Pearl Andrews, however, extended his insinuations to the characters of all of Greeley's friends, and kept at it for twenty years, when his diligence was gloriously rewarded. It was he who as editor of *Woodhull and Claflin's Weekly* broke the country-shaking Beecher-Tilton scandal.

XXIV

Promoting Utopia and a
New Messiah

IN THE LUSH 1850'S SNIPING AT THE
LIBIDINAL DRIVES OF MR. GREELEY
AND HIS FRIENDS MEANT NO MORE
to Stephen Pearl Andrews and Mary Gove Nichols
than did any of the other recreational projects in which
they were voluntarily participating. What they took as
their serious business was the promoting of a new Mes-
siah, this one, for a change, of strictly American origin.
After wandering for a quarter of a century among frontier utopias old Josiah Warren had shown up again in
the more cerebral centers of New York with what he
and his converts took to be a brand new plan for "working out every great problem of Society, without the
destruction of liberty."

If any native-born American had the right to promote such a scheme, it was surely Josiah Warren. He
had the longest apprenticeship in social re-organization
of any American still living. He had been one of the
very first to answer Robert Owen's call when in 1824
that idealistic Scotsman summoned all men of good
intentions to join him in an experiment in communal

living on the banks of the Wabash. Among the motley horde that was drawn to the 30,000 ague-ridden acres that comprised New Harmony, Indiana, by vision of endless free discussions, to say nothing of free food, free clothes, free lodging and the chance to practice free love, Warren had managed to be conspicuous. He did not mind work. He kept his own cottage in repair, allowed vegetables as well as flowers to grow in the plot of ground assigned him, and chipped in and helped the mechanics whom Owen eventually had to hire, to keep the folks of good intentions from freezing and starving to death. When young Robert Dale Owen bought a printing press with the idea of publishing a *New Harmony Gazette*, Warren actually learned how to set up the paper.

Such eccentricities made a profound impression on Miss Frances Wright when on a busman's holiday from her own cultural project in the wilderness back of Memphis—whose inhabitants, quaintly enough, were a handful of boughten blacks—she visited New Harmony. A few years later, having transported her colored communists in howling protest to Haiti and dumped them free, Miss Wright transferred her energy to New York City, then undergoing a virulent attack of evangelism.

The Free Churchers had leased the Chatham Street Theater, ripped out its bar, and were converting it into a bastion of piety from which the moaning, jerking, shrieking followers of Finney were preparing to raid the dense rookeries of the Five Points and unsuspecting drawing rooms on Bleeker Street. As a counter-offensive Frances Wright, that Priestess of Beelzebub, bought the nearest available church, tore up its altar and declared it to be a Hall of Science. To reach a larger audience than the 1,200 which its auditorium would accommodate, she installed a printing press in the Sunday School room, invited the best minds in America and Europe to contribute their ideas to her *Free Enquirer*, and sent for Josiah Warren to come East and publish it for her.

The *Free Enquirer* held Fanny's distractable attention for as long a time as her other enterprises, and when it folded, Warren, who had abandoned his soap factory in Cincinnati in order to join New Harmony unsullied by worldly goods, had become so imbued with the spirit of social uplift that he could not bear to return to the industrial status quo. It was then that he began his rounds of the utopias—giving every type, no matter what its ultimate ideals, unstintingly of his enthusiasm.

He was forever on the move, for the colonies burst almost like bubbles under his feet, until he was driven to the conclusion that there must be one cause for the communal failures. After a protracted period of "laborious study" Warren arrived at the conviction that the evil was money. The inmates of the various Edens had cast off most of the shackling horrors of civilization as it was—the isolate household, the competitive workshop, unwanted children, cooked food, formal education, clothes and common sense—but they still, whenever they had it, used money as the medium of exchange.

It must be then the oppressive power of money that caused even more disharmony in Fourieristic, Swedenborgian and Christian communist circles than it did in the outside world. So after twenty years in the utopian wildernesses Josiah Warren had come back East to spread the word that the "immediate necessity and the last ground of hope for all mankind" was "the complete abolition of all money."

Many social philosophers before and after Josiah Warren have dreamed of a universe run without the necessity of cash. He was prepared to offer exacting proof of the simple practicability of such a plan. For ninety-five days, with the aid of his wife and son and several social-conscious friends, he carried on an elaborate commercial enterprise without a single penny changing hands. He stripped the commodities in which he traded of the false, superficial values that civilization had put upon them and assigned to them their true worth. He evaluated every article which a man might need in the business of living in terms of the most precious of his God-given possessions—time. Since the word "erg" had not then been struck off, Warren called his basic temporal unit "the work hour."

A single work hour had the material worth of a live chicken or a pound of coffee beans. Flour was estimated at twenty hours the barrel, prime beef at ten minutes per pound, sweet milk at fifteen minutes per quart. Fire wood, sawed into handy lengths, came to sixteen hours the cord, sugar to four minutes per pound, heavy work shoes to nine hours and twenty-eight minutes per pair, and ordinary dry goods to two hours, thirty-one minutes and forty-seven seconds per yard.

Using these accurate figures Warren kept a careful record of the entire "expenses" of his own family during the initial experimental period, assessing even such intangibles as the wear and tear on a three room house and the probable wear of clothing. Totting up his figures at the end of the period he found that a family of three could live very well indeed for three months by putting out an average of only one and three quarter work hours a day, exclusive of domestic work.

These were the material and temporal blessings of the new economic system to which Warren gave the name of Equitable Commerce. Its spiritual benefits were much greater. Their liberation from monetary worries had freed the three Warrens from social and moral botherments as well. Their experience, they felt, had raised them not only above squalid standards of the commercial world but "above the state, above systems and above man-made laws." If they could only persuade the rest of mankind to follow their example then for the first time, since civilization began its disruptive struggle with the laws of nature, society would be enabled to make its first groping step toward its eventual harmonious adjustment. By the time Warren presented Equitable Commerce to the liberals of Boston and New York, he was able to state flatly that his new system for re-organizing society "outstrips the sagacity and genius of mankind."

No one in his select Eastern audiences contradicted him on this point, yet his lectures did not have the immediate revolutionary effect that he had expected. His listeners were fascinated by his bookkeeping, but they could not see his simple time store as a complete blue print of the future. Warren, indeed, was in grave danger of suffering the same fate that overcame Howard Scott when he revived Warren's system eighty years later under the name of Technocracy—of being furiously acclaimed by the intellectuals and as quickly dropped—when Stephen Pearl Andrews saw at a glance why Equitable Commerce did not have the wide practical appeal of such systems as—say Esoteric Anthropology.

Warren had been so long in the utopian wilderness that he did not know that the Industrial Revolution, of which men were only dreaming when he went West at the close of the War of 1812, had become a reality. In his re-evaluation of values he had not taken into account the myriad inventions which were the mainstay of this revolution. With the possible exception of the dry goods—which might have been woven on a primitive, hand-driven eighteenth century loom—there was not a machine-made article on the revised equity price-list. Obviously, then, the whole system had been computed on too simple a basis—on the slow manual labor necessary for raising chickens, chopping wood, and hauling flour from a primitive water-mill. Modern industrial speed-up made a more energetic concept of the work hour imperative.

Since Warren apparently was unable to do so, Andrews assumed the task of assigning the correct temporal value to the scientific wonders upon which America's high standard of living was now based—the harvester, the sewing machine, the magnetic telegraph, the rotary printing press, the Otis elevator, the Colt revolver, the safety pin and the paper collar.

There was an even more serious impediment to Equitable Commerce being taken up by the intelligentsia. Being no great shakes as a thinker himself, Warren had put no evaluation whatsoever on the highest type of human labor—progressive thinking. Indeed, the new world order as he had originally outlined it made no provision at all for cultural workers. Poets, actors, painters and philosophers, Andrews pointed out to him, had just as much to contribute to the future as unskilled laborers and just as much right to their one-and-one-quarter work hours a day. They shouldn't be forced to abandon the skills in which they wished to be considered proficient in order to compete with poultrymen, dairy farmers and cobblers. Instead Andrews would work out an equitable wage scale for the cultural workers, so that those who dealt in poetry and prophecy, facts and figures, would be as well taken care of as farmers and mechanics.

And while he was about it Andrews suggested to Warren that he might well change the name of his system. Equitable Commerce stressed only the purely economic side of society's re-organization. Americans could be induced to participate in it much more voluntarily if more emphasis were placed on its spiritual sphere. Since Warren was sure that its adoption would raise all its devotees above civilized society and man-made laws, why not call it Individual Sovereignty?

Under such a concept Andrews would be able to work into Warren's basic principles all the other doctrines in which a true liberal was bound to believe—and make a quicker and more thorough job of it than Dana and Godwin and Ripley and the rest of the appeasers. The new world that Andrews envisioned would be done with logical reconciliations. Individual Sovereignty would lift the onus from inconsistency, conflicts of ideas and general confusion, and make of them positive virtues.

Having gained the bewildered Warren's assent to these ideological additions to his original theory, Andrews now settled to his most difficult task—putting across the Warren personality. As a social thinker the old man had few peers, but as an orator he was a wash-out. He had very little formal education and for more than thirty years had been living in the West. Eastern ears attuned to the golden voice of Emerson, the stirring oratory of Beecher, and Mrs. Mowatt's conscientious anglicisms, found his frontier drawl unpleasant, his halting delivery embarrassing, his grammatical lapses painful.

The resourceful Stephen Pearl Andrews saw how to turn even these deficiencies to account. He adapted to the needs of his protégé the technique Dr. Fishbough had made so effective in the case of the Sage of Hyde Park. He had Warren stop giving lectures and begin to hold Conversations, at which Andrews acted as entrepreneur and chief interlocutor. Andrews, who had given himself the title of Pantarch, now conferred on Warren that of "Euclid of the Social Sciences," and introduced him to his audiences in these words:

"This obscure, plain man of the people is a common-sense thinker, a most profoundly analytical thinker. He may not understand algebra, or the differential calculus, but all social sciences and every beneficent, successful and permanent social institution ever hereafter erected must rest upon the principles which have been discovered and will now be announced by him. There is no alternative."

Andrews not only introduced Warren in this forthright and prophetic manner and asked him the questions which had been skillfully prepared in advance, but shielded him from the jibes of those who under the guise of economy and patriotism sought to re-new the age-old fight for the privileged few against the good of the many. This reactionary group now numbered among its new recruits the editor of the *New York Tribune*. In his bout with free love Greeley had been knocked reeling toward the right and had become almost as conservative as Henry Raymond of the *Times*. His attitude toward Individual Sovereignty, except that it contained not the slightest trace of humor, was strikingly like that which William Watson Webb had adopted toward Fourierism some ten years earlier. But Andrews was a tougher antagonist than Brisbane, and he well knew how to play on Greeley's weaknesses.

When Greeley inquired what would become of the good old tradition of free enterprise if money was abolished in the United States, Andrews replied that Mr. Greeley might as well be stuck "in the heart of Russia for all the comprehension he has, or ever *did* have, of the entirety of the Social Revolution which is actually if not obviously impending; which, indeed, is hourly progressing in our modern society."

And when Greeley asked how we could persuade all the other nations of the world to abandon gold for a temporal standard, Andrews was ready with the perfect retort. "Mr. Greeley has worked hard for *his* money," he pointed out, "so he cannot comprehend in this sublime and simple principle a universal law of equity, which distributes all wealth exactly according to *Right*."

Thus, by a dialectic method with which no one who owns a radio is unfamiliar today, did Andrews silence and shame the critics of Warren's planned economy— to the twittering glee of those who expected to be the first beneficiaries of its sublime and simple principles. Yet, for all that, Andrews and Warren were eighty years ahead of their time. The Democrats came back into power in the national elections of 1852, but in all Franklin Pierce's cabinet and among his closest advisers there was not a single bright young man who urged him to adopt Individual Sovereignty as a blue print for the re-making of America.

XXV

The Sovereigns Seek Harmony
at Modern Times

JOSIAH WARREN'S CONVERTS AMONG THE INTELLECTUALS WERE ALL FOR PUTTING HIS PLANS IN OPERATION right away. Mary Gove Nichols was particularly anxious to try out a social system in which money would be superfluous, for at the moment cash was a pressing worry. Though she was completely satisfied with the drubbing she was giving Mr. Greeley on the spiritual plane, in the continuing controversy over the true meaning of purity and prostitution, even she had to admit that in the material sphere she had been worsted. As soon as her select lady patients discovered that the editor of the *Tribune* shared their own husbands' views concerning the identity of esoteric anthropology and adultery, they fled the Twenty-second Street Water Cure House as from a brothel.

Mrs. Nichols was joined in her desire to start Individual Sovereignty going in the world not only by her husband and Mr. Andrews, but by the Reverends S. C. Hewitt, J. S. Loveland, E. T. Spires and all the other men of God who had deserted Methodist, Presbyterian and Baptist pulpits for spiritualistic rostrums, and then had those lucrative platforms blasted from under them by the Whitney Report—a disclosure of their true relationships with their comely mediums.

This agitated group asked Warren to show them how to begin the moneyless universe right away, basing his directions on his experience with his time store. To them Warren made a confession which he had not thought necessary to explain to the rest of the world. When he had gone to Cincinnati as a young man he had acquired from Nicholas Longworth a sizable tract of land bordering a cowpath. As Cincinnati grew from a frontier village to a city, the cowpath became an important thoroughfare, and by the time Warren was certain that personal possessions were evil things, his property had greatly increased in value. This unearned increment had enabled him to finance his original experiment in planned economy. He had none left for a second try. Even if he had, he felt it would be wrong for him to finance an equity village in which he himself planned to live, for that would give him more power than his fellow villagers who as a result would not feel their sovereignty to be as absolute as his.

Why not then, Dr. Nichols suggested, let the colonizers pool their possessions as was customary in other communal enterprises? Because, replied the Euclid of the Social Sciences, all previous experiments founded on that expedient had failed, and rightly so. The pooling of resources amounted in the final analysis to constant communal borrowing. Even in the simplest transactions the sovereignty of the borrower became less than that of his creditor. Where borrowing was as complicated as it was in a communistic community—where a man subsisted continuously on his neighbors' goods, and they on his—this inequality of sovereignty, this unbalance of power, and its resulting stresses and strains, rendered social relationships even less harmonious than they were in the outer world.

Things seemed to have reached a dead end when Josiah Warren discovered a flaw in his own logic. The inharmonious moods occasioned by continual borrowing were truly oppressive only when debtors and creditors lived in close contact. Distance considerably lessened the psychic strains and stresses. If the source of his borrowing was sufficiently remote, a debtor could feel positively superior to those who footed his bills. Therefore Warren decreed that an entirely harmonious experiment in planned economy could be started on borrowed money, provided every bit of it was "borrowed from outside." Since the United States Treasury was not at this time available for the purpose, those who desired to become "sovereigns over their own" looked around for a private backer. They found one in Edward Linton, who was less interested in social experimentation than in getting a place where the employees of his paper box factory could live adequately on the wages he expected to pay them.

Since thirty years before Robert Owen had discovered

to the tune of $200,000 that men of good will were not necessarily either good or willing workers, a leaven of mechanics had been accepted as an essential ingredient of any communal experiment that expected to last more than a few weeks. The individual sovereigns could fit the paper box makers nicely into their community.

An ideal situation was secured in Suffolk county on Long Island. The tract was forty miles from the "gleaming spires of Manhattan," four miles inland from the ocean, and nothing at all would grow on it but oak so scrubby that it was not even fit for fuel. Mr. Linton supplied some old boards, and where not even a cowpath had been before the first resident of the equitable village of Modern Times erected the community's first dwelling—a ten-by-twelve-foot shanty.

As still more lumber was donated by other outsiders, more and some slightly larger houses were built, until the village contained more than eighty cottages, the progressive school, the co-operative store and, most essential feature of all, the meeting house that was to be used not for sectarian worship but for lectures and discussions. Almost a hundred individuals and heads of temporary families, who had never before owned enough ground to fill a flower pot, could now boast that they lived in their own homes.

Dr. and Mrs. Nichols, Mr. Andrews, and the assorted spirit lecturers, mediums and other intellectuals, were not, of course, expected to work in the box factory or to build their own houses. But they repaid the mechanics who provided for their material wants with an equivalent amount of culture. Warren and Andrews after numerous surveys and computations arrived at the proper value of intellectual labor. They decided that each hour of literary, artistic or educational endeavor was worth exactly sixteen pounds of corn. Etymologists might ponder this medium of exchange.

No corn was grown at Modern Times, of course. But the residents needed some common medium for keeping their records—for computing, for example, how many hours of wood-chopping and water-toting a mechanic should be required to exchange for the autograph of his favorite dead celebrity, obtained from a medium adept in the science of automatic writing. Since money was forbidden on the premises, and work hours could not be spent before they were worked, fertile corn was decided upon as the proper medium of exchange. When it was discovered that a mechanic over the week-end, out on a large cultural binge—attending first a lecture of Fourierism, followed by a symposium on sex, after which he would have to have a new phrenological reading and get his esoteric analysis brought up to date, and then most likely stay up for an all-night session with the spirits—might have to lug about with him several times his own weight in corn, the procedure was reorganized.

Tastily decorated certificates bearing the legend "Corn the equivalent of Labor" and entitling the bearer to five, ten or twenty bushels, or an equitable amount of edible or cultural commodities, were printed and used for trading at the store and gaining admission to the meeting house. To destructive critics from the outside world of the status quo, these certificates looked suspiciously like twenty-five and fifty-cent notes and dollar bills; loyal Modern Timers refused to recognize the resemblance.

All non-mechanical residents of the community could discuss authoritatively all the philosophies that had gone into the making of the all-over theory of Individual Sovereignty, and most of them did so without any urging. But though the meeting house resounded with disputes and arguments at all hours, the cultural activities, though considerably confused, were not uncoordinated. So that the sovereignty of each would be as absolute as that of every other, every individual was given a special department—dietetics, mesmerism, education, associationism, politics, pathetism, labor problems, nature, theological discussion, phrenology, peace, dress reform—over which he reigned supreme—or until his authority came in conflict with that of a sovereign in a related field.

Because of her experience Mrs. Nichols was made co-ordinator of sexual activities. And yet because of her lack of experience Miss Rosemary Yewell, the trance medium, was put in charge of children's activities. The Pantarch, who acted in the Jeeves-like role of a sort of sovereign's sovereign, had estimated from a survey that "9 out of 10 children are much better reared by somebody else than either parent." Since Miss Yewell had been entirely without contact with the material world since her thirteenth birthday, when the spirits claimed her, she was just the person to counterbalance the adverse environmental conditions from which the children of the mechanics suffered, because before coming to Modern Times they had lived in isolate households with both parents. Another point in Miss Yewell's favor as directress of the progressive school was that during her speaking trances she had acquired a natural facility for Five Points epithets from some of the tougher spirits.

Mrs. Nichols in her department initiated some excellent reforms. By executive order she abolished the wedding ring, and substituted in its stead the "fresh piece of string." Should a lady show up at the common eating place with a piece of string newly tied in a love-knot about her little finger, this would mean that she was announcing that she had changed love-partners during the previous night. Everyone else would immediately look for the gentleman whose smallest digit was similarly adorned. But no one, not even the children who were encouraged to ask questions about everything else under the sun, including sex, could hazard a ribald query about string—not even the size of Andrews' reputed hoard.

There was not as great an increase in the incidence of children among the sovereigns as would have been the case had their unrestrained love practices been followed in the outside world—thanks to Mrs. Nichols' former husband, now become her paramour, who was also administrator of health. Dr. Nichols had developed his wife's happy phrase—that if a woman has any right in this world it is the right to her own ovum—into a "law of nature, repeated throughout the animal kingdom."

"If she has the right to decide who shall be the father of her children," he reasoned, in words that seemed to have been written only yesterday, "she has an equal right to decide whether she will have children and to choose the time to have them." And since she alone has the "right to decide whether her ovum shall be impregnated," she must also be granted the privilege of determining those "circumstances which justify the procurement of abortion, or the untimely expulsion of the embryo, or foetus." And so in the meeting house Thomas Nichols informed his fellow workers about those topics so dear to the hearts of all liberals—the proper spacing of a family, the safe period, the most up-to-date methods of birth control and the surest methods of abortion. "A surgical operation," he assured his prospective patients, "is the simplest and the one accompanied by the minimum of danger."

With such stirring reforms as these, Modern Times could boast of being the only community in the world completely free of prostitution, courts of law, rum-shops, sectarian churches, policemen and jailhouses. It did not long lack publicity. It was Mary Gove Nichols, not surprisingly, who caused reporters from New York and special writers from papers as distant as the *Cincinnati Gazette* to descend on the idyllic community.

As a visible token of their individual sovereignties the colonists eschewed alike the current fashions of the world as it was and the drab uniforms too often associated with communistic experiments. Only the recognized sponsor of dress reform—and the children of the progressive school who had to be prepared to live in the more equitable climate of the new world their elders were wishing for them—could go completely naked. The others thought up exclusive costumes symbolic of themselves. The ladies wore skirts of varying lengths— from below the ankle to above the knee—signifying their progress in casting off the moral shackles of the world as it was. Mary Gove Nichols, making manifest the Pantarch's certainty that she combined a woman's wonderful intuition with a masculine understanding of general principles, wore a large, floppy, flower-bedecked hat on her head, and tight breeches on her general principles. She wore the costume not only about the premises but to meet the train.

Commuters along the route were, unaccountably, more impressed by her swaggering backsides than by the total bareness of Mr. Hewitt, the dress reformer. They talked about her on the train and in the oyster bars after they got to town. One of Mr. Greeley's leg men, overhearing their bawdy chatter, knew who it was they must be describing. With his fellows from the

Herald and the *Police Gazette* he took the next Long Island train.

The colonists greeted the press cordially and staged special cultural exhibits for them. But with the crassness characteristic of their calling, the reporters gave little space to the lectures on Fourierism and the pathetistic demonstrations. They played up instead two exceedingly puzzling deaths. Miss Hattie Eager, the pregnant medium of Mr. Fairbanks, specialist in Nature, had succumbed to a diet of arsenic, an idiosyncrasy in which her operator encouraged her under the logical belief that any craving by a woman in her particularly natural condition must be more natural than Nature itself. The second death was that of the sponsor of food reform who had literally died for her position. In her research to find the perfect diet, she had set herself to live a whole year on unsalted beans, and unexpectedly expired before the eleventh month was up.

The reporters also found Mrs. Nichols excellent copy. Her catalogue of all the evils attributable to indissoluble marriage, and her description of how well she had the sexual situation in hand at the colony, caused Modern Times for many years to be referred to by non-spiritualist ministers throughout the land as "that cesspool in the nostrils of all believers in true morality."

Being ridiculed and denounced by the outside world only made the Modern Timers admire one another more than ever. When the colony finally folded Josiah Warren was able to declare that it alone, among all the similar institutions that dotted the landscape of America in the middle nineteenth century, had not been brought to ruin by internal disharmonies. It failed because the outside world had not adopted its self-evident principles. But most important—Mr. Linton lost his factory and his shirt in the crash of 1857.

The Nicholses, however, warned by the spirits, had beaten the gun and gone West to Cincinnati where they caught up on their writing, neglected in the strenuous activities of communal living. Mary Gove once more set down her life story, this time for a change all in one coherent volume. It was surprisingly, since she promised to tell all, the most restrained of her works, touched in places by an almost reactionary urbanity. Her husband declared that it would have had a much better sale than "that book by Mrs. Stowe" had it not "been virtually (or virtuously) suppressed by the New York publishers in consequence of the onslaughts of Greeley, Raymond and company, and the conservative press."

When its sales remained considerably less than those of *Uncle Tom,* its author felt the necessity of starting another utopia. The Nicholses accompanied by half a dozen followers set out for Yellow Springs where, unluckily for them, lived another famous refugee from New England.

A few years before Horace Mann had held views precisely like those of Mary Gove on all the wonderful new ideas. The work-while-you-learn college for less-than-privileged youth which he had come to Ohio to found had already been denounced as dangerously radical by some sections of the conservative press. He could not afford to have his youth project endangered by even geographical association with a Nichols' free love colony. Mann denounced his erstwhile fellow liberals as fiercely as yesterday the followers of Stalin denounced the followers of Trotsky. The Nicholses got no recruits in Yellow Springs and very little to eat. Had it not been for the temporary haven of a nunnery, they might have starved to death.

Their goal was now New York, and the Nicholses attained it by a circuitous route. Not having the money for train fare across the continent, they worked their way down the Mississippi, Dr. Nichols doing itinerant healing in the river towns until they reached New Orleans. There they took a sailing ship back to New York.

For all her buffetings Mary Gove Nichols arrived in New York more confidently than she had sixteen years before. She had taken the town once and she had learned the trick. Now all she need do was to take up her life where it was ended in her autobiography and which remained her peak moment—the establishing of her Water Cure. But she reckoned without the change that had come over the liberals in the past few years.

All the wonderful cosmic energy that had been used for discovering, improving and wrangling over all the new ideas, was concentrated now in the one deep angry movement of Abolition. And in 1860 even the liberals knew that Abolition was but a wrathful synonym for War. Being unable, for all the star-got force they directed against it, to stem the onrush, Thomas L. Nichols and Mary S. Gove Nichols uprooted themselves from the land which once held all their hopes of a brave new world. Weeping, they sailed for London.

THE END

Set in Linotype Caslon Old Face
Format by A. W. Rushmore
Manufactured by the Haddon Craftsmen
Published by Harper & Brothers
New York and London